CARNEGIE INTERNATIONAL 1991

VOLUME II

THE CARNEGIE MUSEUM OF ART, PITTSBURGH

RIZZOLI, NEW YORK

Curators: Lynne Cooke and Mark Francis   **Carnegie International 1991**   The Carnegie Museum of Art

Pittsburgh, Pennsylvania   October 19, 1991 – February 16, 1992

Michael Asher	Mike Kelley
Richard Avedon	Louise Lawler
Judith Barry	Ken Lum
Lothar Baumgarten	Allan McCollum
Christian Boltanski	John McCracken
Louise Bourgeois	Boris Michailov
John Cage	Lisa Milroy
Sophie Calle	Tatsuo Miyajima
James Coleman	Reinhard Mucha
Tony Cragg	Juan Muñoz
Richard Deacon	Bruce Nauman
Lili Dujourie	Maria Nordman
Katharina Fritsch	Giulio Paolini
Bernard Frize	Stephen Prina
Dan Graham	Tim Rollins + K.O.S.
Ann Hamilton	Richard Serra
Richard Hamilton	Thomas Struth
David Hammons	Hiroshi Sugimoto
Huang Yong Ping	Philip Taaffe
Derek Jarman	Christopher Williams
Ilya Kabakov	Christopher Wool
On Kawara	

Carnegie International 1991
October 19, 1991–February 16, 1992

Major corporate support for the *Carnegie International* exhibition and catalogue is provided by Mobay Corporation, Agfa Corporation, and Miles Inc.

Additional funding is provided by income from The A. W. Mellon Educational and Charitable Trust Endowment Fund for the Pittsburgh International Exhibition and by the National Endowment for the Arts, the Pennsylvania Council on the Arts, the Howard Heinz Endowment, and the James H. Beal Publications Fund.

Grants have also been received from Association Française d'Action Artistique (AFAA), Ministère des Affaires Etrangères, The British Council, The Canada Council for the Arts, The Cartier Foundation for Contemporary Art, Citiparks, Compass Management and Leasing, the Embassy of Spain, the Flemish Community of Belgium, The Henry Moore Foundation, Iberia Airlines of Spain, Professional Photography Division–Eastman Kodak Company, the Trust for Mutual Understanding, and the Western Pennsylvania Conservancy.

Published in 1991 by
The Carnegie Museum of Art,
4400 Forbes Avenue,
Pittsburgh, PA 15213-4080

ISBN: 0-88039-023-9

Trade Edition published in 1992 by
Rizzoli International Publications, Inc.,
300 Park Avenue South, New York, NY 10010
ISBN: 0-8478-1499-8

Library of Congress Catalog Card Number
90-657322

Editors
Lynne Cooke and Mark Francis

Copy Editor
Ann Bremner

Design
Bruce Mau

Design Associates
Alison Hahn, Kathleen Oginski
and Nigel Smith

Typesetting
Archetype

Printed in Canada
by Bradbury Tamblyn and Boorne Ltd.

Photographic materials used for Volume II of the 1991 *Carnegie International* catalogue have been provided by Agfa Corporation.

Acknowledgments

During the final moments of preparation for the 1991 *Carnegie International*, leadership at the corporate sponsor of the exhibition changed. We wish to express gratitude to Helge Wehmeier, recently appointed president and chief executive officer of Bayer U.S.A. Incorporated, who gave his enthusiastic support to the exhibition. We also are grateful to Sande Deitch, recently appointed executive director of Bayer-Mobay Foundation, who worked closely with us during these months.

In addition to those individuals recognized in Volume I, we wish to acknowledge the following people who have helped to create the 1991 *Carnegie International*:

Chris Ackerman
Roland Augustine
David Bancroft
James Barnhart
Gail Barringer
Douglas Baxter
Marie-Claude Beaud
Martin Beck
Jenny Becker
Donald Bell
Gianfranco Benedetti
Tom Bills
John F. Bittner
Sir Alan Bowness
Betty Brazell
Jeff Breland
Ann Bremner
Warren Brennan
Joyce Broadus
Coosje van Bruggen
Sharon Bruni
Benjamin H. D. Buchloh
Jacqueline Burckhardt
Charles Burges
John Caldwell
Ed Cannon
Juan Cassiers
Janine Cirincione
Ornette Coleman
David Conrad
Maria Corral
Robert Croneberger
Chantal Crousel
Bice Curiger
Byron Davenport
Dr. Mary Dawson
Jane Dayton
Hermin Dehennin
Ray H. DeMoulin
Chris Dercon
Richard Desroches
Mario Diacono
Leslie Dick
Ron Diulus
Deborah D. Dodds
Anthony d'Offay
Ulrich Domrose
Rita Donagh
Shelley Dowell
Joan Duddy
Patrick Duffy
Fred Escher

Fei Dawei
Ronald Feldman
Milton Fine
Sheila Fine
Gust Flizanes
Eric Franck
John E. Frohnmayer
Gerlinde Gabriel
Larry Gagosian
Colin Gardner
Gary Garrels
Jeff Gerson
Suzanne Ghez
George Gilpin
Allen Glatter
Richard Gluckman
Ann Goldstein
Marian Goodman
Edythe Goodridge
John Goodwin
Derek Gordon
Jerry Gorovoy
Digby Green
Marcia Gumberg
Stanley Gumberg
Alison Hahn
Dave Hasch
Philip Heidinger
Annick Herbert
Anton Herbert
Max Hetzler
Greg Hilty
Fred Hoffman
Winter Hoffman
Antonio Homem
William A. Huber
A. C. Hudgins
Xavier Hufkens
Phil Hundley
Mary Jane Jacob
John Jacobs
Diana Janetta
Peter Janetta
Christos Joachimedes
Jörg Johnen
Jane Johnston
W. Juwet
Emilia Kanevsky
Peggy Jarrell Kaplan
Julia Kaufmann
Hiroko Kawahara
Karen Kelly

Lenders

Michael Asher
Richard Avedon
Judith Barry
Dove Bradshaw
John Cage
Sophie Calle
The Carnegie Library of Pittsburgh
Leo Castelli Gallery
Philip Chiaponne and Mary Brennan
Tony Cragg
Galerie Crousel-Robelin BAMA
Richard Deacon
Diab Data AB
Anthony d'Offay Gallery
Gordon Douglas
Ronald Feldman Fine Arts, Inc.
Rosamund Felsen Gallery
Bernard Frize
Gagosian Gallery
Marian Goodman Gallery
Ann Hamilton
David Hammons
Fred Hoffman Gallery
Huang Yong Ping
Jablonka Galerie
On Kawara
Mike Kelley
Mary Jean Kenton
Nicole Klagsbrun Gallery
Sarah-Ann and Werner H. Kramarsky
Mr. and Mrs. Mark Le Jeune
Louver Gallery
Luhring Augustine Gallery
Luhring Augustine Hetzler Gallery
Ken Lum
Allan McCollum
Vijak Mahdavi and Bernardo Nadal Ginard
Boris Michailov
Robert Miller Gallery
Lisa Milroy
Marvin and Elayne Mordes
Galerie Nelson
Maria Nordman
Stephen Prina
Andrea Rosen Gallery
Galleria Lia Rumma
Mr. and Mrs. Keith L. Sachs
Gaby and Wilhelm Schürmann
Richard Serra
Marsha Skinner
Sperone Westwater
Emily and Jerry Spiegel

Hiroshi Sugimoto
Micheline and Charly Szwajcer
Philip Taaffe
Gallery Takagi
The Trustees of the Tate Gallery
O. M. Ungers
Walker Art Center
John Weber Gallery
Thea Westreich
Christopher Wool

VOLUME I

Contents

Scaife miniatures, The Carnegie Museum of Art, Pittsburgh

Change of State: An Exposition
Lynne Cooke

In the warm shade of the orange tree, leaning back against the silk pillows of the divan, Sinbad half dreams of the telling of the voyages. At first the telling had made the voyages so vivid to him that it was as if the words had given them life, it was as if, without the words, the voyages had been slowly darkening or disappearing. Thus the voyages took shape about the words, or perhaps took shape within the words. But a change had been wrought, by the telling. For once the voyages had been summoned by the words, a separation had seemed to take place, as if, just to one side of the words, half-hidden by their shadows, the voyages lay dreaming in the grass. In the shade of the orange tree Sinbad tries to remember. Are there then two septads of voyages, the seven that are told and the seven that elude the telling? Before the telling, what were the voyages? Unspoken, did they exist at all? Are there perhaps three septads: the seven voyages, the memory of the seven voyages, and the telling of the seven voyages?...[1]

I.

Tucked into the center of The Carnegie, virtually in the seam of a wall in what may be the smallest gallery in the museum, is a series of miniature rooms.[2] Three windows offer views onto replicas of the dining room, library, and living room of a house near Pittsburgh from the mid-twentieth century. Tellingly, however, the rooms are furnished in a period style reminiscent of eighteenth-century England. Several other windows open onto displays of miniature domestic furnishings. Presented to the museum in the 1960s, more than half a century after The Carnegie opened its doors, this singular collection is located most appropriately at the juncture between the Hall of Sculpture and the Hall of Architecture and adjacent to the Museum of Natural History. Whether these miniatures are original artworks or copies, whether they belong to the aesthetic or the anthropological domain is not altogether clear, though their most immediate counterparts are to be found in the habitat groups in the natural history galleries nearby.

As in the conjunction of dioramas with vitrines containing stuffed specimens in the natural history museum, so the methodology of display in these miniature rooms stands in strict opposition to that employed in the fine art galleries upstairs, where objects stripped from their contexts are exhibited as individuated specimens in sequential isolation. There furniture is placed on pedestals like functionless sculpture; paintings are arranged chronologically and generally in accordance with national origin. In this layout curatorial decisions concerning placement and arrangement indicate, in part, the value or significance attributed in scholarly terms to the object. These dual modes of display exemplify the two principal approaches to the presentation of material artifacts: on the one hand, treated as individual autonomous treasures, and on the other, recontextualized as part of a socio-cultural context, as habitat groups, as dioramas, as period rooms. Subtending these display techniques are quite distinct aesthetics and ideologies. Yet both approaches developed in service to the act of collecting, integral to which is, as James Clifford puts it, "a gathering up of properties in arbitrary *systems* of value and meaning.... The inclusions in all collections reflect wider cultural rules, of rational taxonomy, of gen-

der, of aesthetics."[3] In quite different ways a number of the artists who devised projects for the 1991 *Carnegie International* addressed the issue of the museum's holdings, making apparent the arbitrariness of all taxonomies while illuminating the values and ideologies that inform them.

Lost Objects is made from casts taken from molds of dinosaur bones in the collection of The Carnegie Museum of Natural History, which includes some five hundred dinosaur specimens, mostly single bones. As casts, *Lost Objects* epitomizes a scientific practice whereby composite skeletons may be formed for exhibition from different examples of the same species, even by mixing casts alongside fossilized bones. A concern with scientific research as well as with public education and entertainment (plus a shrewd sense of self-promotion) clearly motivated Andrew Carnegie when he bestowed casts of the *Diplodocus Carnegii* onto museums as far flung as Moscow and Mexico City soon after he had sponsored the field trips which unearthed this rare discovery for the Museum of Natural History in Pittsburgh.[4] Located in the Hall of Sculpture midway between the Hall of Architecture, with its plaster copies of western masterworks, and Dinosaur Hall, dedicated to the Jurassic giants, Allan McCollum's project invokes questions of classification and taxonomy, reflects upon different ways that knowledge is acquired and transmitted by means of models, copies, and replicas, and addresses the diverse ways in which collections are formed and apprehended. Still mysterious, almost fantastic, dinosaurs are the perfect vehicles to bridge the gap between art and science, the former concerned with the unique and original artifact, the latter with the representative, with genera and the natural.

An anthropological approach leavened with connoisseurial finesse underpins Richard Deacon's reinstallation of choice three-dimensional items from different departments of The Carnegie Museum of Art. Three categories of object — functional, decorative, and sculptural — were to be presented on communal bases alongside a model of what once was widely considered the high point of western culture, the Parthenon, which, however, proved impossible to move from the Hall of Architecture. Beneath David Smith's *Cubi XXIV*, a "mat" was inserted to create a quasi-interior setting for a work that the American artist preferred to exhibit outdoors. The other two bases offer rafts for objects shipwrecked between competing museological claims, as if testifying to the widely held belief that "disciplines make their objects and in the process make themselves."[5] Deacon's juxtaposing of objects according to materials and methods of manufacture highlights the interpretive framework presupposed in selecting, de- and recontextualizing, and through that speaks to the curatorial process in its cognitive as well as connoisseurial character.

Sophie Calle focuses on the varied histories that lie behind domestic artifacts, histories that are often masked, occluded, or otherwise neutralized by museological display. Her interventions in the Bruce Galleries, which house the decorative arts collections, invoke the cardinal ways in which memory operates, notably how memory adopts narrative modes in its reconfiguring of an anonymous item, transforming something representative back into a singular entity, turning specimens into relics. Regardless of whether the personal narratives she proposes are autobiographical facts or authorial fictions, they offer a verbal historicizing that plays ironically with the tropes of periodization and contextualization typically offered in museums of history and folklore. The transforming of an object into a legendary exemplum through contingency and the accidents of history is fulsomely acknowledged in history museums; the inverse tends to occur when similar items enter the decorative arts collections of an art museum. Yet little that is intrinsic divides forensic evidence, archival material, precious artifact, fetish, or icon: the shifting character of the respective roles depends largely on the nature of the framing tools. Moreover, identity is neither natural nor innocent: antiquities, curiosities, art, souvenirs, monuments, and ethnographic objects have all been differently defined and differently valued at different times.

Calle's second project, a reconstruction of the thirteen works stolen from the Isabella Stewart Gardner Museum, spotlights the idiosyncrasy in that museum's approach to display. Illogical and willful by any standard, the Gardner collection remains in perpetuity as determined by the founder, who not only designed the installation but lived in it. In being drawn, like this patron, to a private fixation on objects — one very different from the rule-governed, tasteful, and systematic habits of the "good" collector — Calle indicates something of the "savage" or deviant relationship that is presupposed but negated by a proper or normative relationship. Both of Calle's projects bear witness to the acuity of Susan Stewart's claim that "the boundary between collection and fetishism is mediated by classification and display in tension with accumulation and secrecy."[6]

Sorted into different typologies and spread over some twenty folding tables like items in a church bazaar sale or data in an ethnologist's laboratory, Mike Kelley's stuffed animals — a taxidermist's bad dream — offer themselves to anthropological scrutiny. The accompanying documentary photographs, together with a painting using an "illustration" style, instill that effect of distancing so critical to the interpretative

Sigmund Freud's study, Vienna 1938

and comparative study of any culture and thus reinforce the impression of a society under examination.[7] Aptly likened to "baby statues," stuffed toys become the paradigms "from which children are supposed to learn that the world is bright, secure, and friendly, and that the fact of the human body is manageable."[8] No longer cute and adorable, in their dirty and worn state these battered handcrafted knickknacks now signal other, less readily acknowledged, levels of meaning: levels that pertain to the underbelly of the high culture or to unredeemed and unredeemable subcultures. All such references are of course customarily laundered or censored from consideration in the fine art arena, for its supposed role is to elevate, educate, and entertain in that order.

The very traits of diversity and miscellany that serve in modern eyes to impair the serious intent of collections were essential elements in a program whose aim was nothing less than universality. The compendious character of an encyclopedic museum, such as The Carnegie, had its roots in the *wunderkammer* and *kunstkammer* of earlier ages, in collections which brought together antiquities, natural wonders, singular artifacts, coins, armor, and other eccentric discoveries in a heterogeneous ensemble.[9] Order or systematizing was generally the product of highly arcane systems, often of systems allied with mystical thought, with mnemonics and personalized cosmologies, hence with a symbolic rather than a didactic method, one which centered on man rather than on nature per se, and on man attributing order to nature. Such symbolic schemes of arrangement had certain affinities with Giulio Camillo's Theater of Memory, itself but one of a number of attempts to form a coherent idea of reality by superimposing abstract schemes on it.[10] Judith Barry's packets of cards, which are piled into a stand topped by a hypothetical model of the Theater of Memory, combine a contemporary advertising-design ethos with reference to older systems of learning and knowledge such as Camillo's. Freely available to audiences entering the building, Barry's *Ars Memoriae Carnegiensis* offers a guide, in the guise of a game, for mapping The Carnegie at large and for apprehending something of its diverse collections.

Taking a tangent on the museum, John Cage sites his contribution to the 1991 *International* at the Mattress Factory, an institution dedicated to the collection and presentation of installation work. Cage's decision to work collaboratively, together with his reliance on chance for both the selection and the arrangement of the seating elements and of his own artworks and those by three other contributors, counters conventional exhibition procedures, while alluding to the interplay of contingency and design in the formation of any collection. Conflating the willful and the serendipitous in these changing daily displays brings to mind the inimitable phrase Francis Bacon employed in 1594 to characterize the formation of *wunderkammer*, the prototypes for encyclopedic museum collections: "whatsoever singularity, chance, and the shuffle of things hath produced."[11]

II.

The designs of certain of the central exhibition rooms in the 1907 Carnegie Institute building — one notably based on the Parthenon, another on the Mausoleum of Halicarnassus — invoke architecture as a symbolic signifier of meaning.[12] Elsewhere in the building, especially in the entrance lobbies and vestibules, notions of public ceremony and entertainment come to the fore through the employment of styles similar to those found in hotel foyers, department stores, or railroad stations. The extension designed by Edward Larrabee Barnes and inaugurated in 1974 functions in a somewhat analogous way in that its foyers and entrance halls recall the architecture of contemporary corporate headquarters, hotels, and shopping malls. By contrast, its top-lit galleries offer the requisite setting for the autonomous modernist art object, and with that a detached, disinterested scrutiny.

Dan Graham's concern with the social exchange at the basis of viewing art, with, that is, an exchange formed within the modes of the spectacle and the spectacular, has led him to prefer the so-called ancillary spaces of the museum, the foyers and lobbies, to the galleries proper. Here, where informal behavior, appointments, and rendezvous occur, far from the hushed and solemn exhibition spaces occupied by absorbed, contemplative viewers, the activity of looking can be foregrounded in a nondidactic but eloquent manner. *Heart* was designed for one of the principal entrances to the art museum, the point of transition from exterior to interior, the site where visitors congregate and orient themselves. Graham's work speaks to conditions of spectatorship in its use of two-way mirrored glass as much as in the form and image it takes. As lighting conditions change, the reflections alter so that the viewer sees him- or herself at the same time as seeing through to others in the distance, inside the work or passing by. Seeing is, however, a far from simple or straightforward activity as the distortions and anamorphic refractions attest. Moreover, it is inseparable from the imprinting of one's body on that which is seen, a participatory if highly voyeuristic act. The beholder's viewpoint is thus revealed as never neutral, disinterested, transcendental, disembodied, or objective, but always culturally grounded, rooted, produced, and filtered by social and historical circumstance. *Heart* makes visible the ways in which the process of looking unfolds while perforce becoming complicit with it.

Yet how the gaze operates depends on the framing conditions as well as on the conditions of spectatorship. For as the form of Graham's pavilion further makes evident, the museum plays a plethora of roles, some of which are congruent with those of corporate headquarters, hotels, and other public spaces whose foyers signal their acts of public service and self-publication in highly ambiguous terms. The IBM atrium in New York, for example, can barely be distinguished from the lobby of a contemporary museum building, where space increasingly is devoted to allied functions — of sales, illicit liaisons, etc. — recalling in passing the extraneous activities that also occurred in the peripheral recesses of cathedrals, buildings to which Graham's works pay an indirect homage.[13] Reversing the traditional hierarchy of roles operating in older museums he turns the galleries into satellites, into mere appendages.

As they approach that ideal modern form of the pure white cube with all specifying detail removed, gallery spaces become increasingly abstract. The dissolution of the specificities of site, and the consequent blurring of categories of place and time, often results in artworks becoming disembodied images, free-floating in a timeless ether. Richard

Charles Willson Peale, *The Artist in His Museum* 1822

Serra's work counters this, speaking as much to the character of the actual site as to the act of apprehension as a bodily-based activity. Seeing in this sense recalls Merleau-Ponty's dream of a meaning-laden imbrication of the viewer and the viewed in the flesh of the world, that is, seeing is an experientially based relationship grounded in actuality. *Judith and Holofernes*, a site-specific work, transforms the mute, cubic volume of the gallery. It metamorphoses what is a clear symmetrical relationship at a visual level into an electrified tension at an emotional one through a finely wrought relation of scale, size, and visual weight. Just as this particular work literally cannot exist elsewhere so the experience of it cannot be replicated, duplicated, or otherwise meaningfully simulated.

If Richard Serra's work contends with the normative modern gallery space, Tony Cragg's might be said to presuppose it. In an adjacent room Cragg capitalizes on what may, with equal plausibility, be considered not the passive but the harmonious neutrality of these well-proportioned spaces. The trio of sculptures he presents employ two traditional materials, stone and bronze, plus steel, a material closely associated with Pittsburgh's industrial past. The forms, however, are far from traditional in the associations they engender. Cragg invokes the conventions of sculpture to question mankind's changing, and dangerously precarious, relationship with the fundamentals of the material world. Characterizing his works as "thinking models," and drawing on diverse traditions and methods, he implicitly treats the museum as a research institute.[14]

Historically, there have been two principal roles for the art museum: treasure house and so storehouse, academy and so research center. Both have their roots in European models. But in America another conception of the museum flourished in the nineteenth century, one with a populist basis. Exemplified first in Charles Willson Peale's Philadelphia Museum, then in P.T. Barnum's American Museum, the museum as pretext for popular entertainment continues to thrive in the twentieth century, as seen for example in the recent founding of a museum devoted to Barbie Dolls.[15] Affirmed in Dan Graham's approving assertion that the Dutch architect Rem Koolhaas discerned the basis of the American museum in Coney Island, this typology also forms a central reference point in much of Bruce Nauman's recent work. Using motifs such as clowns, taxidermists' models, and cast body parts reminiscent of those found in wax museums (and hovering on the borderline between freakish aberration and scientific orderliness), his compositions are charged with a gallows humor mingling horror and delight. This, in turn, provides an entrée into what is a searingly bleak, Beckett-like vision of human relationships, a vision that like its vernacular predecessors challenges credulity as it challenges intelligibility.

The "perfect" equilibrium between modernist architecture and modernist art was first and arguably best achieved in Mies van der Rohe's exhibition pavilions, notably the Barcelona Pavilion of 1929. Where Graham salutes while subtly revealing the complexities integral to Miesian precepts of transparency, clarity, order, and harmony, Lothar Baumgarten pays homage to their flexibility and durability as operative standards and viable models. Inserted into the structure of a late Mies building, the Richard King Mellon Hall of Science at Duquesne University, Baumgarten's terms are actually as relevant to the disciplines of science, and to the activities of research, as to architectural theories. Their embeddedness in the culture at large, and the values they represent, are celebrated in a statement that embodies the beauty and rigor of this aesthetic at its pinnacle in a form inherently at one with

André Malraux and *Le Musée imaginaire* 1954

the architectural style rather than applied as a decorative appendage. Whereas a classic line of names of (male) scientists, artists, and musicians rings the fascia of the 1907 Carnegie Institute building, in Baumgarten's work the denominative figural reference has been, appropriately, replaced by the abstract and symbolic.

In both its basis and its very structure, architecture is at once visible and invisible within the museum. Sited in what is usually the first of the temporary exhibition galleries at The Carnegie Museum of Art, Thomas Struth's images of architecture offer, through the medium of photography, another discourse on site, spectacle, the act of viewing, and the ways that culture is shaped by the built environment. The group of smaller photographs of buildings shot in what appears to be a straightforward archival manner is offset by two larger, strikingly beautiful images of crowd scenes, one of an intersection in central Tokyo, the other of the Pantheon in Rome. Seemingly disordered, the random grouping of people is, rather, subject to a notion of order quite different from those which are integral both to architecture and to Struth's documentary practice. The conjunction of the two sets of photographs speaks to a social process in which the visual arts no longer have an inherent or meaningful relationship with architecture, and where the viewing of architecture in turn increasingly takes place through the medium of another artform, namely photography. If the problematic divorce of art from architecture leaves the museum by default the preferred home of artists, their residence there may be somewhat uneasy. The sentiments of the German artist Ludger Gerdes would be echoed by many others: "The mother [of the arts] is making efforts to become a whore, the children should stay in the orphanage of the museum; at least this place shouldn't be turned into a brothel."[16]

III.

The uniformity of the museum audience, or, alternatively, the tailoring of the audience to certain sets of values, assumptions, and presuppositions, usually goes unremarked, though the components of the art public are readily known — and not just to sociologists. Ken Lum points to the cultural assumptions and ethnic and other biases presupposed in regular museum visitors in his poem paintings whose form approximates more closely that of the banner or scroll than that of the quintessential western fine art object, the oil painting on canvas. In choosing texts in five languages — Inuit, Japanese, Maltese, Nepalese, and Vietnamese — which are likely to be unfamiliar or inaccessible to the vast majority of the viewers of this show, Lum makes evident certain of the presuppositions that most visitors bring to the museum. Those interpretative biases that are often quite unconsciously focused on objects from other cultures, whether Ming vases or Benin bronzes, together with the speciousness and falsity of claims about the universality of visual objects are thereby foregrounded. His works require a recognition of difference, specifically in this case of the nomadic character of certain societies whose culture is portable or even immaterial in its expression and hence not collectible. Pitched against Malraux's celebrated notion of the "Museum without Walls" — the *musée imaginaire* — in which all of human visual culture is purportedly instantly and equally available, Lum seeks to particularize and recontextualize.

First *Annual Exhibition*, Carnegie Institute 1896

He speaks to the loss that de- or recontextualizing brings, and to the inevitable limitations that attend any viewpoint, and any position.[17] If the search for a transcendental common ground is revealed as highly problematic (for notions of universality are usually predicated on the irrelevance of context and contingency), what equally requires recognition is the shifting liminal borders both between and within national communities and the fact that it is still difficult to think of the politics of cultural identity outside questions of nationality, notwithstanding the strong presence of those whose histories are expressed in such hyphenated compound terms as African-American, Aboriginal-Australian, Chinese-Canadian, Soviet-emigré…. By questioning in what coinage cultural exchange occurs, Lum asks how the traps of nationalism may be avoided in the search for the right to represent oneself, to have one's own ethos and ethnos.

The complementary component of Lum's project is some thirty (mostly bilingual) poetry books, from which the five texts that comprise the banner-paintings were selected. These books have been donated to the eighteen branches of The Carnegie Library of Pittsburgh. On the spine of each may be found the call number for the same book in a library in its country of origin together with the reference number used in the Pittsburgh system. Lum here indicates a possibility for significant exchange, for the dissemination of information and knowledge across boundaries, and for the free flow of information necessary to cultural and social parity and equality. Offering simultaneous translation, the library is not a treasure house but an academy (unlike the museum which has a dual identity); as such, it is able to recognize and negotiate difference rather than a fixed otherness, and to establish a shifting inbetweenness that permits the circulation of information. The result is a more difficult and differential commonality, a cross-referencing that requires participation in order to operate.

Poised between the library, the Museum of Natural History, and the Museum of Art, Christopher Williams' work too seems to address the types of information and categories of knowledge sought in the various branches of such a resource center as The Carnegie. Presented in display cabinets, Williams' artifacts, over-sized books based on the scale of Audubon's classic publications, employ signifying systems divested of reference points, and matheses and taxonomies devoid of keys. On the one hand they invoke such precedents as cabinets of curiosities whose systems of ordering knowledge were arcane, hermetic, and often ultimately personal; on the other they speak to the fragility and even arbitrariness of all constructed systems of classification and presentation which, being rational, generally come to be considered natural. Through their endless deferral of meaning the fallaciousness of such beliefs is demonstrated, and skepticism and doubt replace uncritical, passive consumption.

Subverting the authority of the written word has a different implication for the Chinese exile Huang Yong Ping. If his work is informed by a political perspective, it equally pays homage to Joseph Beuys, at once the propounder of a philosophy of social sculpture and the champion of the creativity of each individual as an artist, and to the book works of the British artist John Latham. Set in the very room in which the *International* was initiated in 1896, this project eloquently manifests the problematics behind the idealistic impulses in Carnegie's conception of that show, while simultaneously restoring the encoded dictates of published opinion back into living matter.

The concept of the book as the site of imaginary fictions and flights of fancy seems remote from that of the book as a repository of information or as the voice of authority. The public aspect comes to the fore with the latter whereas privacy seems to be the ideal presupposed for the reading of fiction. The solitude that accompanies this immersion in novels typically takes place within a domestic realm. The milieu of interior space mimes, as Susan Stewart notes, the creation of both an interior text and an interior subject.[18] Tribute is paid this in the donation of twenty-one texts by Tim Rollins + K.O.S. to the Homewood branch library in each of which a page has been "illuminated." Since these books are not otherwise identified, the illuminations will mostly be encountered by the unsuspecting reader in the privacy of his or her immersion in the tale. By contrast, in the works that Rollins + K.O.S. exhibit in museum spaces, a book is usually filletted, dismembered and laid out to form a ground on which the painting is then executed, a process which acknowledges that the space opened up by the novel also belongs to the realm of shared cultural memory. However, for this particular version of *The Temptation of Saint Antony*, a subject on which they have been working for a decade, they chose to concentrate on a single section of Flaubert's text, perhaps partly to facilitate the incorporation of students from Pittsburgh into the collaborative enterprise. (Their choice of this particular text was conditioned by the fact that the Museum of Art owns a haunting painting on the same theme by the Belgian symbolist James Ensor, which was shown in the 1938 *International*.) Fragmented, but reiterated over and over, the polyphonic litany of the forty-two panels rings with individual and collective responses to their central tenet: "Death is then a mere illusion, a veil, masking in places the continuity of life./ But since substance is one, why are forms so various?"

James Ensor, *The Tribulations of St. Anthony* 1894

As domains aspiring to encyclopedic completeness the library and museum have long been aligned. In ancient Alexandria they were a unified entity; when the British Museum was founded in the late-eighteenth century the library was an integral component. In conjoining a library, art collection, and natural history museum (and music hall) Andrew Carnegie was following a well-established model, if one that by the beginning of the twentieth century had begun to seem outmoded. More than just the separation and specialization of different functions and discourses had intervened: the very notion of encyclopedic total-ization had been brought into question. Perhaps no more brilliantly barbed account of this can be found than in Flaubert's great novel *Bouvard and Pécuchet* (1881), a text that has recently become the sub-ject of renewed interest. Eugenio Donato succinctly describes the fruits of the two protagonists' pursuit of all of human knowledge through systematically exhausting its diverse modes: "Having begun with the dream and hope of a total, finite, rational domain of knowledge, they come to realize that not only is knowledge as a given totality unavailable but also that any act of totalization is by definition incomplete, infi-nite and everywhere marked by accident, chance and randomness."[19] That Bouvard and Pécuchet finally abandon all attempts at compiling an encyclopedic library and a museum, assumed to be the ultimate prin-ciple of reality, and revert to random copying is at once peculiarly fitting and deeply unsettling. In the interplay between the library and museum in the work of artists such as Lum, Huang, and Rollins + K.O.S., as in their weighing of their different realities against each other, a radical qualification of earlier models of the treasure house and academy is annunciated and a new if more limited potential discerned.

In contrast to the encyclopedic museum with its diverse origins, the museum of modern art has its roots in the modern era coinciding with the rise of a modernist art, an art that sought for itself autonomy and a neutral, separate space in which to confirm that identity. This was in effect a sanctified space, a space which in turn brought about the institutionalization of art. If the neutral white cube has become one of the hallmarks of the twentieth-century presentation of art,

equally persistent has been a desire to reconnect, to break down the barriers, to undermine and seek alternatives to those models of auton-omous artwork, dispassionate (or disinterested) viewer, and neutral con-tainer. Diverse motivations have led artists to move into new arenas, to find alternative spaces, new alliances, and novel strategies whereby art may again be submerged into everyday "life" — as evidenced in the Dadaists' cabaret and the Constructivists' agitprop or in the Situa-tionists' dérive and haçienda. More recently, since the later 1960s, such ideals have led to the dematerialization of the art work, to the crea-tion of temporary site-specific works, and to the establishment of alternative venues.

The last thirty years, however, also have witnessed a boom in museum building unprecedented since the nineteenth century, together with the consolidation and subsequent institutionalization of so-called alternative venues, the kunsthallen and ICAs, and a reconsideration of notions of site in even their most conventional guises. With the much vaunted death of the avant-garde, and the loss of serious alternative roles or positions, the museum is increasingly perceived as the rightful inheritance of the artist, who now demands an annuity before it is too late. (Here a contrast must be made with others for whom the art market as distinct from the art institution is perceived as the principal agent or determinant and hence the focus of study.)

The critique of the museum as institution, its history and ideology, that burgeoned in the 1960s has now garnered a rich legacy and an ongoing dynamic. Louise Lawler typically presents her work in sites within the museum that cross over from the hallowed gallery arena to low-status intermediary spaces used for functional, practical, or tran-sitional ends. In this project Lawler uses photography not as an art medium per se but for documentation. Since all strategies of display are necessarily artificial, display itself may be considered a form of theatrical artifice, mutable and contingent. Resiting the same photo-graph three times, each time with a different statement, Lawler trans-ports the image from within the temporary exhibition area to the threshold of the permanent collection and to a "non-space" by the telephone cubicles, where posters and other reproductive works nor-mally hang. Each text and each site inflect differently what is seen, and how it is read, especially since Lawler treats words less as captions than as elements of visual display in their own right. The multiple identity accorded every element is further enriched when one notes that the photograph installed in the exhibition proper depicts the very site on which it is placed, albeit at a previous moment when the per-manent collection occupied that gallery. The adjustments needed to accommodate the *International* are signaled wittily by the fact that a Richard Deacon sculpture in the permanent collection but now in stor-age is glimpsed as reflection in her image while the glass covering that image itself refracts views of Deacon's pedestals (themselves sub-suming other items from the permanent collections) created for the current exhibition and located just in front of Lawler's image. If the for-mat of the huge rococo motif announcing the "Squid in its own Ink" has a public character of a kind befitting the title placed at the com-mencement of a major exhibition, the paperweight located discretely in the corner requires a closely focused, intimate viewing of a sort very different from that conventionally associated with the blockbuster show.

The object of scrutiny in Lawler's photograph is a Heinz ketchup box, in her paperweight a portrait of Andrew Carnegie: both are the work of Andy Warhol, a native of Pittsburgh. That this ketchup carton is a container now contained, an everyday manufactured object treasured in splendid isolation, but equally, in solitary confinement, neatly puts a further gloss not only on the role of the artist in an anthology exhibition, and on curatorial practice in general, but on the staging of this show in this particular socio-cultural and historical situation.

Like Lawler and Dan Graham, Michael Asher works to reveal the social and material conditions of art's practice and function, conditions which, according to theorist Douglas Crimp, it has been the modern museum's function to dissemble.[20] In their art such enquiry is not incompatible with the venue of the museum but rather serves to alert the viewer to the operations of that locale. Asher's acronyms in plaster are situated in the Hall of Architecture among plaster casts of canonical works of the past. If few artists today boycott the museum, preferring to examine the institutional protocols governing art's meaning from within, the focus of their critiques has greatly widened to accommodate contradictions and ambiguities rather than being marked by refusals and absolutes, as Asher's work devoted to engineering and material standards, and the hazards of toxic materials, eloquently attests.

IV.

Museum collections comprising specimens create an illusion of an adequate representation of the world by first excising objects from specific contexts (historical, cultural, or intersubjective) and then making them "stand for" abstract wholes. A system of classification is elaborated for displaying the object so that the reality of the collection itself, its coherent order, overrides the specific histories of an object's production and appropriation. Dioramas and habitat groups, by contrast, attempt to reconstitute the original milieu. In their desire for immersion in authentic experience, many artists find the environment or installation a perfect vehicle, for each treats the object not as a fragment but as a component situated in a free-floating totality, albeit an imaginary or metaphorical reality rather than one preexisting outside the aesthetic arena.

Pioneered in American natural history museums, dioramas and habitat groups were constructed from the early years of the twentieth century as part of the zeal for greater realism. This realism, which Umberto Eco identifies as quintessentially American, focuses on a faithful representation, a lifelike rendering, a process of mimesis or painstaking imitation. For him, Americans are preoccupied with the "real" copy of the reality to be represented, and hence with a philosophy of immortality as duplication: "to attain the real thing one must fabricate the absolute fake," he maintains.[21] Disneyland and other theme parks have supplanted the populist museum of old, but museums of high culture still vigorously promote a (hyper) realism through the ongoing construction of ever more real dioramas. The monumental Egyptian Temple of Dendur, recently reerected in majestic splendor in the Metropolitan Museum of Art, is sited, tellingly, almost adjacent to the Chinese Garden Court from the Ming Dynasty, which has been aptly

described as "an outstanding, indeed hyperbolic, demonstration of the search for absolute authenticity in all material details."[22] However real such wonders, their historical dimension and, with that, their historical significance become, as Stephen Bann contends, almost entirely subsumed into the spectacular and the exotic. It is precisely this that Ilya Kabakov plays upon in his installation, a "reconstruction" of an abandoned orphanage. In Kabakov's work, worthless scraps and discards, detritus that carries no visual interest and so seems of purely documentary relevance, become ironically the stuff of great value. Fantasy and literalism, invention and reconstruction, are so interwoven here that the historically insignificant becomes inextricable from the aesthetically resonant.

The kind of contextualizing that Kabakov seeks in his installation presupposes a notion of mimesis as the touchstone of reality. For Louise Bourgeois *vérité* not *vraisemblance* is the measure for what might be defined as psychological truth. In her *Cells* objects, sometimes made, most often found, are contextualized not through recreating an appropriate historical setting but by means of fictive or imaginary environments and sites. These *Cells* embody a variety of different emotional states and senses relating to pain, hysteria, frustration, loss, and longing, to obsessions and compulsions and other states too nuanced or inflected to be easily labeled with words. Some *Cells* can only be witnessed from outside, others invite interaction. In each case recognition of the threshold is crucial. To lose one's borders is to be in chaos: formlessness and disorder supervene.

For Susan Stewart "the nostalgic is enamored of distance, not of the referent itself. Nostalgia cannot be sustained without loss. For the nostalgic to reach his or her goal of closing the gap between resemblance and identity, *lived* experience would have to take place, an erasure of the gap between the sign and the signified, an experience which would cancel out the desire that is nostalgia's reason for existence."[23] This effect of suspension is ideally possible in the sanctuary offered by the art museum. Here collective memory, cultural memory, and even personal memory can be constructed by artifice, rather than being generated by lived experience. Whereas Bourgeois' works invite supplementation by narrative discourse which articulates the play of emotion, Juan Muñoz characteristically shields himself from explication of the discursive through the adoption of a tableau format or related form of staging, via the use of masks or of thrown voices in echo and mimicry, and via the persona of surrogates and marginals as proffered by the ventriloquist's dummy and the dwarf. An impassioned admirer of Houdini, Muñoz posits the artist as someone like a stuntman or double who no longer mimes but lives the ceremony of his perception of the world according to preordained tropes. The certitudes of social identity and position embodied in the eighteenth-century conversation pieces of, say, Arthur Devis, have been perilously undermined in Muñoz's project, for these figures pivoting on their hemispherical bases may adopt any position, but adhere to none. The fragile and tenuous connections made by the viewer in linking the play of glances into a temporary whole is always and necessarily rudely shattered by the physical motion of moving into and through the physical space.

The melancholia of exclusion ambiguously evoked in Muñoz's work presupposes a model of the world as a stage, and of the viewer as surrogate actor: "When the spectator walks across the floor," Muñoz contends, "this stage quality induces in him some of the awareness of the actor or, at least for a while, it puts off his stance as a distant onlooker."[24] However, this is but one of several models generated by installation work. For Lili Dujourie, if the museum is a sanctuary or refuge for contemplative experience, then the spaces of the museum can become equivalents of the spaces of the mind. Through the introduction of false perspective, for example, her stagings subtly disrupt the coherence of the viewer's vantage point, intimating that the appropriate position to adopt is not an actual but a projected one.

Where for Dujourie the site of artistic creation is, firstly, the mind, for Reinhard Mucha it is literally and figuratively the atelier: the result is that the studio and the exhibition gallery become interwoven as subjects. In *The Wirtschaftswunder* Mucha has literally made the present out of the past, by creating a new work from part of the past history of the building that became his studio and then recontextualizing this work alongside other works from his first exhibition, including a piece, *Untitled (Wand)*, that itself documents a student work, his contribution to a diploma show of graduates from Klaus Rinke's class at the Düsseldorf Academy. In so doing, Mucha reveals the creative act to be one which entails a labyrinthine filtering of the past in ways that render its products, the specimen and the relic, indistinguishable from each other. He reconfigures certain relics of the past into autonomous artworks that he then recontextualizes into an installation, which, in the context of the museum, can be read as a kind of period room whose ultimate subject is the biography of the artist as maker. The exhibition process and presentation are drawn together with the exhibits into something that forms a collective history.

Paul Valéry lamented the death of the artwork on entering the museum, and the impossibility of its resurrection in the hodgepodge of a miscellaneous collection. Marcel Proust adopted a diametrically opposite position, finding in the museum the ideal context for the activities of involuntary memory.[25] In their sober abstinence the rooms of the museum symbolize for Proust the inner spaces into which the artist withdraws to create the work of art. Only when severed from the living order in which it once functioned is the spontaneity of the artwork released, he believed: there it becomes a kind of optical instrument offered to the viewer in order that he or she make self-discoveries perhaps not otherwise possible. As an actual situation not an illusory depiction, moreover, a situation which excludes all else from its purview, the installation has a kind of presentness, even hyperreality, at once rooted in actuality and yet removed from ordinary experience. Yet from this very fact of removal grows the danger that the work may become either neutralized or, alternatively, subverted into the spectacular and exotic. It is this threat that leads certain artists to work outside the museum or to adopt an ambivalent relation to it. According more weight to the process than the product is another means adopted to subvert the ways in which the work of art is metaphorically put to death and so becomes a specimen as it enters the storehouse of the past.

Ann Hamilton has worked in a variety of venues making tempo-

rary site-specific pieces which have no life beyond the circumstances of the exhibition in the conviction that art is an ongoing process rather than a finite product. In devising work that is highly labor intensive, and that therefore requires the collaboration of others, she takes a philosophical as much as a practical stance: "A museum makes it possible for viewers to return to its collections again and again, but it also sets things apart from the continuum of life — takes them out of circulation and places them in the stasis of the perpetual past," she contends. "Making site-related work — work that is ephemeral and constituted of organic materials — is part of retracing the path back towards art that is among the living and therefore among the dying."[26] In her installations this has often taken the form of having agents or actors as integral parts of the piece; on other occasions it has involved living systems, vegetal and/or animal, and on others documentation that is historical, diaristic, and scientific, that addresses what has become extinct, or irretrievably past: "If collecting is about the removal of objects to a hermetic context," she argues, "then art that exists in the seams can introduce and remind us of all that cannot be preserved."[27] In *offerings*, these means are deployed to create a situation that aims to affect the viewer at a level prior to language, that draws on recognitions that are somehow earlier or more primal through their rootedness in the body and thus their connections with other living systems. For Hamilton, the distance engendered by speech which seeks to name, to analyze, to interpret, serves as a means to control, whereas "the body has so much wisdom in it, if only we would pay attention to it."[28] As manifest in her thought and art, and in that of Bourgeois or Muñoz, poetics is ineffable, being viscerally based.

Moving not only outside the building but outside the institution, Maria Nordman addresses the unsuspecting visitor who may experience the work without recognition of its identity as art. She situates her project not as anti-art but as art operating in terms of the public arena, specifically in this case, the city. Reminiscent of the original dwelling as imagined by Abbé Laugier, Nordman's schematic house with its permeable walls offers an image of reconciliation between private and public spaces, nature and culture. Open to the elements and to passing view, and thus permitting ready passage between subjective experience and worldly experience, between the self and the city, Nordman's structure reaffirms what Richard Sennett defines as the ancient value of exposure, for it was this which in antiquity allowed the individual to find his or her orientation, to keep a balance between the public and private self, to be "centered."[29]

In contrast to Nordman and Hamilton whose ambivalent attitudes to the museum have to do with the neutralization that may occur when art is institutionalized, David Hammons concentrates on the role of the maker over the process or the product. Speaking from a position which acknowledges the marginal without itself being marginalized, he recently stated: "I feel it is my moral obligation as a black artist to try to graphically document what I feel socially," adding, "I'm speaking to both sides."[30] As in most of his installations, Hammons began here with the site, the physical character and the identity of the particular space, and perhaps, too, with the tenor of this exhibition, much of which was already in place by the time he arrived to make his work.

Transporting artworks for an early *Annual Exhibition*

First, two walls were transformed, painted with a decorative stencil in a pattern used in residential interiors; the third took on the traces of a basketball session. Placed on a stand at head height is an old and venerable paint-shaker, a wryly oblique reference to an archetypal (Abstract Expressionist — read heroic, white, male?) artist and to a basketball player.[31] As the ball begins to vibrate its sound is overlaid by a tape of music by James Brown, creating a loud and proud image of black identity, aspiration, and achievement. At once a metaphorical portrait, a challenge and a greeting, *Yo-yo* alludes to areas of expertise, to standards of measure and relevance outside the traditional framework of the American art museum.

V.

> ...in this long digression which I was accidentally led into, as in all my digressions (one only excepted) there is a master-stroke of digressive skill, the merit of which has all along, I fear, been overlooked by my reader, — not for want of penetration in him, — but because 'tis an excellence seldom looked for, or expected indeed, in a digression; — and it is this: That though my digressions are all fair, as you observe, — and that I fly off from what I am about, as far and as often too as any writer...yet I constantly take care to order affairs so, that my main business does not stand still in my absence.... Digressions, incontestably, are the sunshine; — they are the life, the soul of reading; — take them out of this book for instance, — you might as well take the book along with them....[32]

Casts and other forms of reproduction, ranging from engravings to photographs, were the most common means of amassing a collection of great masterworks for many museums founded in the later nineteenth century. With regard to the art of the present, in the case of The Carnegie Museum of Art at least (and this was perhaps not atypical), the focus was placed squarely on painting. Until the late fifties the *International*, the major show of contemporary art undertaken by

the museum on a regular basis, was devoted to painting, and, as with many twentieth-century collections, The Carnegie Museum of Art's (exhibited) collection consists primarily of paintings. Consideration of the current place and role of painting seems to have become an inevitable component in any *Carnegie International*.

Debates as to the ongoing relevance, vitality, and centrality of painting have bedeviled much of the twentieth century. In recent years they seem to be always couched in terms of the limitations and liabilities that attend painting.[33] Imputing to painting an embattled position, they are epitomized in the following exchange between the German painter Gerhard Richter and the art historian Benjamin Buchloh. Asked if the representational function of painting and its self-reflexivity were brought together in his work "in order to show the inadequacy and bankruptcy of both," Richter replied, "Bankruptcy no, inadequacy, always."[34] A model of probity and seriousness in his enquiry, Richter embodies a contradictory stance, that, if not directly influential on the younger painters included here, nonetheless sets a standard of critical engagement. Yet for a number of other artists the issues (formerly) addressed by painting or deemed particular to painting can now only be addressed tangentially. Hybrid forms, for example, may serve as a better basis of enquiry, or alternatively, those photographically based media that have supplanted many of the traditional functions of painting may now not only usurp its former role but become its correlatives.

John McCracken's recent pieces, presented on the wall, partake of both painting and sculpture while being neither. Their illusionistic character is not a depicted illusionism but one that results from and responds to the specifics of the situation, to the actual fall of light on highly reflective planes of color, and to the shifting positions of the spectator moving around the object. This slippage between the actual and the illusory serves metaphorically to enact a transition from the real to the non-real, and since the principal means effecting these changes are light, space, and time, this metaphor becomes grounded in notions of the super-real, of metaphysics, even of a mystical orientation. Encountering the un(fore)seen is central to the potency of McCracken's works; the very antithesis, the already seen, fuels Katharina Fritsch's, though she might concur with his avowal, "I don't believe *in* the material world, only *through* it."[35] The point of genesis for much of her art lies in memory, albeit in its more elusive corners and interstices. The identity of these works as paintings is in some respects only incidental: they are more catalysts than pictures, and more reminiscent of icons than of windows onto the world.

Whereas neither Fritsch nor McCracken might be identified as painters, this is not the case with Bernard Frize, Lisa Milroy, Philip Taaffe, or Christopher Wool, for whom therefore the legacy of past painting must weigh differently. None of these four young artists is engaged with subjective expression nor with personalized experience. Their analytical approach leads to an investigation of inherited languages, vernacular idioms, preexisting signifying systems, and routinely familiar decorative schemata, which are manipulated through patterning, printing, stencilling, chance procedures, repetition, and collage as well as via the brushstroke. Painting is understood as a conventional, historical language, one that carries, at least by now, the narratives of specific intentions and desires, of nameable authors and established discourses.

Recognition of the inherently metaphorical nature of all imagery and form, abstract or not, underpins their work as it does that of McCracken and Fritsch, yet they rely far less on the conveyance of meaning via intuition, association, and feeling: theirs is in a sense a much more structuralist emphasis. For Milroy this becomes inseparable from a concern with painting as grounded in language, in the ability to name, to identify, to describe. Yet given that this takes place in the realm of the visual, it presupposes a different type of scanning from the linear one peculiar to reading. Allied to this is the recognition that mapping, placing, ordering, sorting, and framing are as much a means to imparting meaning as is the evocation of the individual object through style, technique, and form.

To Frize it is axiomatic that the maker must extricate himself from the activity, that he (or she) must relinquish his signature mark. Treating painting as a productive arena for research, he playfully yet methodically emphasizes the painting process itself, and its materials and technologies, even to the extent of hunting down specialized or novel tools and instruments.

For Wool, for whom the problematics of meaning are also a key concern, this is nowhere more urgently evident than in his text-based works where the bold stark lettering demands attention in the manner of signage, yet given its syntax/composition impacts equally as image. Unlike signage, however, painting no longer has a clearly defined social role, and any measure of its effectuality must be inconclusive, rendering it a dubious enterprise at best. Notwithstanding appearances to the contrary, Wool's art refuses to deliver a message, making meaning dependent on the spectator's psychological and cultural associations.

In his latest paintings, Philip Taaffe invites a reconsideration of the social implications of ornamentation. Since the advent of abstraction early in the twentieth century, decoration has been rigorously eschewed. A painting that was decorative supposedly forfeited significant content: it was considered inherently trivial, shallow, ornamental. In what has become now a routine vilification of decoration its purpose is seldom questioned: it has become a sanctified shibboleth. Taaffe expounds on the fact that in certain Mediterranean and Middle Eastern cultures ornament serves to veil something that must remain only tangentially known, that can only be glimpsed but never directly apprehended. This allows him, by extension, to speak metaphorically to the forming of content in contemporary painting. Although the assimilation of decorative forms from other cultures over a period of time has usually stripped them of their original meanings, turning them into generalized form, Taaffe begins to rehabilitate cross-cultural migration: if not inverting the process he at least undercuts something of the free-floating quality of the unattached signifier. In the astonishing cultural mix that marks Naples, his adopted home, a mix that has not produced an emptying out of meaning but a complex palimpsest, one that is simultaneously vital and decadent, ultra-contemporary and unforgettably ageless, lies the promise, methodological as well as aesthetic, for a transformation in contemporary painting.

But perhaps the most surprising adherent to painting in an age that is frequently characterized in terms of the ubiquity of its technologi-

cal media, is Richard Hamilton in whose long and varied career painting has always played a paradoxically central place. Hamilton's forays into new developments in design and technology have been more far reaching than those of many artists, yet perversely he has never surrendered his sense of himself as a painter, even when employing imagery culled from the mass media and then using computers to organize and collate it.

The one area that Hamilton has always eschewed, pure abstraction, forms the basis of a survey of twentieth-century art in Stephen Prina's series entitled *Monochrome Painting*.[36] Having previously recontextualized other artists' work, Prina here subjects his own to a process of inventorying and classification. Reducing the elements of an earlier exhibition and its appurtenances, together with a subsequent suite of prints, to a uniform medium (wash drawings) and format (determined by size and shape alone), Prina restructures and re-presents his work according to a very different yet rational methodology: he inventories one after another of these now homogeneous entities in a logical, sequential order reminiscent of that used in card cataloguing then exhibits them hung salon style.

It could be said of Giulio Paolini's work as it has been of Prina's, "In the broadest sense…it is cultural authority itself that is the object of restructuring."[37] Taking the picture as his vehicle, Paolini subjects the viewing of art to quizzical scrutiny, largely by playing on the shifting positions embodied in Cartesian perspectivalism. Without relinquishing his (ironic) stance as a painter — *pictor sum* — Paolini reveals what is widely viewed as empirically true and universally valid to be contingent and constructed, and thus no more the acme of human achievement than the now deposed classical languages which it partially replaced and into which his project is discretely inserted along the frieze of a faux-classical temple.

Engaged, like Paolini, with the rhetorical conventionality of sight, and acknowledging that the gaze is as much a social fact as it is a physical operation, James Coleman examines the discursive determinations integral to vision, indicating their part in the production of subjectivity and in their own production as part of intersubjectivity. The vehicle through which this occurs is a stereotypical romance involving a quartet of players. The medium is slide-tape. If the conventions of representation used here derive partially from painting and film, the nature of photography as an indexical medium of reproduction is subtly established through the contextualizing of the fragmentary narrative in a palaeontology laboratory. In this complexly layered work, who and what is the subject of the gaze, what is background and what foreground, and where the conventions and roots of representation reside become seminal issues. That these have currently become central questions in the study of the painting of the past is far from irrelevant.

VI.

In his laconic but incisive comment that fossils must be the oldest photographs, Coleman points to the way that photography offers a trace of a moment lost irretrievably. "History has no periodic table of elements, and no classification of types or species; it has…no theory of temporal structure," George Kubler asserts.[38] Photography is today the most ubiquitous means to record history, but it does not answer fully the question of how to deal with the past if history is to be more than a repository of material artifacts and images, if it is also to embody memory — collective and personal memory.

In Hiroshi Sugimoto's project, *Time Exposed*, that which is preserved in the photograph, the transitory instant, has been captured from one of the most elemental sights, the sea and sky framed symmetrically. The fine quality print, normally the subject of stringent conservation controls, is here allowed to weather in the elements, even to the point where it will virtually disappear, and so takes on the marks of time in yet another sense. As the repository of the past the museum preserves earlier endeavors to record what Sugimoto sees as basic human experiences: his project at once acknowledges and connects with this aspect of the museum's role and yet countermands it.

The repetition of cyclical time, the urgency of linear time — both preoccupy Tatsuo Miyajima whose darkened installations serve to disorient the viewer to the point of removing all sense of physical location and whose digital numbers tick off the measurement of something unspecified. Miyajima's aim is to focus on what might be considered an abstract, even universal, level. The vastness of time symbolized on the one hand in the traces of dinosaur remains and contrarily on the other in the futuristic impulses of his digital counters suggest degrees of temporality far outside those of human history, as much the subject of the science museum as of the art museum.

It is most fitting that On Kawara's *Today 1966–90* should be positioned in the Hall of Sculpture amidst imported (classical) and native American languages, the latter memorialized in Lothar Baumgarten's *The Tongue of the Cherokee* (1988). Painted in the language of the country in which he was present on that day, each of Kawara's works is when displayed an existential statement. When stored in its specially crafted box alongside a page from that same day's newspaper from the city which gave the work its particular language, each is accompanied by the specifics of historical occurrences perceived from a particular vantage point.

Christian Boltanski's strategy of constructing a fictive archive of the *Carnegie International* from its inception in 1896 to the present serves at once as a sharp reminder of the vicissitudes of history and also as a sobering lesson to artists, critics, and curators alike. As an entity the museum necessarily deals with the past, with its preservation, its reconsideration, its transformation into the present. The stark objective record of the past that the archive offers stands in diametrical contrast to the way history is recalled or recreated via memory, as indicated in Boltanski's other installation, from the series *Les Suisses morts*. Enlarged to over life-size, the photographs of heads lose definition. The resulting generic vagueness coupled with the fact of a public presentation encourages putative identification, based on the expectation that such a presentation must imply that these anonymous people are public figures, celebrities, even media stars. The context forces competing and contradictory readings and the projection of identity, stature, and meaning quite contrary to what is or may be known to be the case, for Boltanski makes no secret of the fact that he has gathered his subjects from the obituary columns of a Swiss newspaper, the

standardized format of the image paying vivid tribute to the operations of death as the great leveler.

By contrast, Richard Avedon imbues the anonymous participants in the crowd with an existential, if not heroic, weight. In his evocation of New Year's Eve in Berlin in 1989–90, a significant historical moment is registered through the play of emotion in what began as documentary shots but were extensively reworked into a carefully studied composite statement.[39] By resorting to dramatic presentation, Avedon seeks an equivalent for the emotional experience he underwent while never ignoring the methods by which historical memories are fabricated and imprinted.

The manufacturing of memories of significant events by the media is the subject of a very different type of scrutiny in certain works by Boris Michailov in which the rhetoric of received tropes and of public spectacle is insidiously undermined and, simultaneously, the privacy of ordinary individual experience is imbued with affectionate dignity and regard. The relationship between the collective and the private is necessarily experienced very differently by Michailov, living in a culture where freedom of artistic expression has until recently been vigorously proscribed. Working in his native Kharkov in a laboratory where family and other snapshots were brought to be copied, adjusted, and hand-tinted, he began making additional copies for himself, copies which he then colored in a more subversive spirit. The "poor" character of his prints, a product of necessity, serves as an eloquent metaphor for the unofficial status of this work, its lack of a public context, while its subject, paradoxically, seems to be the methodologies by which other identities might be given, or forged.

That photography should be the principal medium used by artists to address the past, to confront issues relating to death, history, and memory is perhaps no accident: the irony of it, poignantly captured in the statement by one of Coleman's protagonists — "I am afraid of time racing or stopped. Polaroids fading…" — is lost on none of these artists.

VII.

Christopher Wool's Situationist quote suggests that the modern audience has been divested of its home, turned into nomads by, on this occasion at least, an exhibition which takes them not only through the institution as a whole, but across the city and, at least metaphorically, beyond: to other places, other situations, other worlds.[40] The circuitous pathways crisscrossing the exhibition, then played out on another scale in serpentine meanderings around the city, refuse any didactic, or even linear ordering. No single point of entry marks the beginning of the show, and there is no conclusion to its labyrinthine unfolding. Neither one kind of exhibition space nor one type of museum prevails.

The purpose of the traditional museum building was to make available a coherent attitude toward the cultural artifacts of the past and toward history. As any certainty that history forms a coherent pattern is undermined, so the function of the museum building and with that of the exhibitions it houses will change. The eclectic structure that constitutes Carnegie Institute is both literally and metaphorically a testament to contradictory paradigms, notably to the grafting of a modern

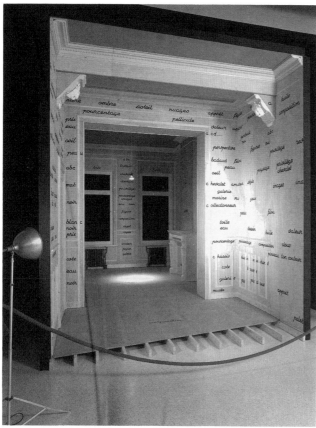

Marcel Broodthaers, *La Salle blanche* 1975

art museum onto an encyclopedic model; its contemporary relevance may lie precisely in this pointing to the resulting lack of cultural coherence. Even if the audience may no longer have a home, the artists have not necessarily forfeited theirs.

1. Steven Millhauser, "The Eighth Voyage of Sinbad" in *The Barnum Museum* (New York: Plume, 1991), p. 119.

2. The Sarah Mellon Scaife Miniature Collection, consisting of eleven showcases, was first put on view in 1968. Similar miniatures, most notably the Thorn Rooms at the Art Institute of Chicago, can be found in other museums.

3. James Clifford, "Objects and Selves — An Afterword" in George W. Stocking, Jr. ed., *Objects and Others: Essays on Museums and Material Culture* (Madison: The University of Wisconsin Press, 1985), pp. 237–238.

4. See Helen J. McGinnis, *Carnegie's Dinosaurs* (Pittsburgh: The Carnegie Museum of Natural History, Carnegie Institute, 1982), pp. 13–17.

5. Barbara Kirschenblatt-Gimblett, "Objects of Ethnography" in Ivan Karp and Stephen D. Lavine, eds., *Exhibiting Cultures: The Poetics and Politics of Museum Display* (Washington D.C.: Smithsonian Institution Press, 1991), p. 387.

6. Susan Stewart, *On Longing: Narratives of the Miniature, the Gigantic, the Souvenir, the Collection* (Baltimore: The Johns Hopkins University Press, 1984), p. 163.

7. For a discussion of taxidermy as a visual art occupying the mid-ground between sculpture and photography, including a comparison of taxidermy, as a three-dimensional mode of mimetic reproduction, to the film frame, both of which offer "a frozen temporal section in the incarnation of art and science," see Donna Haraway, "Teddy Bear Patriarchy: Taxidermy in the Garden of Eden, New York City, 1908–1936," *Social Text* (Winter 1984–1985), pp. 20–64.

8. James Lewis, "Mike Kelley: Beyond Redemption," *Artforum* (Summer 1991), p. 74.

9. Both in their own right and as models, *wunderkammer*, or cabinets of curiosities, have recently aroused much interest among artists, as demonstrated in the exhibition in the central pavilion at the Venice *Biennale* of 1986. Fictional museums and collections have also recently been the subject of considerable interest, evidenced in such exhibitions as *Museums by Artists*, Toronto, Art Metropole, 1983, *Histoires de musée*, Musée d'art moderne de la ville de Paris, 1989, and *Feux pâles*, Bordeaux, CAPC Musée d'art contemporain, 1989. The influence of Marcel Broodthaers' fictional museums and related projects, including *La Salle blanche* (1975), and Marcel Duchamp's *Boîte en valise* (1936–41) is critical in this regard.

10. See Frances A. Yates, *The Art of Memory* (Chicago: The University of Chicago Press, rpt. 1989 [1966]), for a fuller study of Camillo's Theater of Memory and other approaches to schematizing memory.

11. Francis Bacon quoted in "Introduction" to *The Origins of Museums*, eds. Oliver Impey and Arthur Macgregor (Oxford: Clarendon Press, 1985), p. 1.

12. See James D. Van Trump, *An American Palace of Culture: The Carnegie Institute and Carnegie Library of Pittsburgh* (Pittsburgh: Carnegie Institute, 1970), pp. 1–21, for a fuller study of the Carnegie Institute building and its architectural references.

13. See Lynne Cooke and Mark Francis, "A Conversation with Richard Serra and Alan Colquhoun" in Volume I of this catalogue, p. 30.

14. "Tony Cragg Interviewed by Lynne Cooke" in *Tony Cragg* (London: Arts Council of Great Britain, 1987), passim.

15. See Edward P. Alexander, "Charles Willson Peale and His Philadelphia Museum: The Concept of a Popular Museum" in *Museum Masters* (Nashville: The American Association for State and Local History, 1983), pp. 43–78 and Alice Kahn, "A Onetime Bimbo Becomes a Muse," *The New York Times*, Sunday, September 29, 1991, Section H, pp. 1, 24–25.

16. "Ludger Gerdes interviewed by Trevor Gould," *Parachute* 44, (July/August 1987), p. 15.

17. Homi K. Bhabha, "Simultaneous Translations," forthcoming in *Art in America*.

18. Susan Stewart, *On Longing*, p. xi.

19. Eugenio Donato, "The Museum's Furnace: Notes Towards a Contextual Reading of *Bouvard and Pécuchet*" in Josué V. Harari, ed., *Textual Strategies* (Ithaca: Cornell University Press, 1979), p. 214.

20. Douglas Crimp, "The Art of Exhibition," *October* 30 (Fall 1984), pp. 49–81.

21. Umberto Eco, "Travels in Hyperreality" in *Travels in Hyperreality* (San Diego/New York/London: Harcourt Brace Jovanovich, 1986), pp. 4, 6.

22. Stephen Bann, *The Clothing of Clio* (Cambridge: Cambridge University Press, 1984), p. 91.

23. Susan Stewart, *On Longing*, p. 145.

24. Quoted in Steven Henry Madoff, "Sculpture: A New Golden Age?," *Art*

News (May 1991), p. 120.

25. This analysis is indebted to Theodor Adorno's essay, "Valéry Proust Museum" in *Prisms* (Cambridge, Massachusetts: The MIT Press, 1981), pp. 175–185.

26. Ann Hamilton and Kathryn Clark, *view*, (Washington D.C.: Hirshhorn Museum and Sculpture Garden, 1991), n.p.

27. Ibid.

28. "a conversation with ann hamilton Hugh M. Davies and Lynda Forsha" in *ann hamilton* (San Diego: Museum of Contemporary Art, 1991), p. 63.

29. Richard Sennett, "Introduction" to *The Conscience of the Eye: The Design and Social Life of Cities* (New York: Alfred A. Knopf, Inc., 1990), pp. xi–xiv.

30. David Hammons in M. Berger, "Issues & Commentary II — Speaking Out," *Art in America* (September 1990), p. 80.

31. This description reflects Hammons' original configuration of *Yo-yo*. The stand was subsequently lowered to about waist height.

32. Laurence Sterne, *The Life and Opinions of Tristram Shandy* (London: Penguin, 1985 [1759–67]), pp. 94–95.

33. Three examples from critics with quite different positions may exemplify this. Yve-Alain Bois, "Painting: The Task of Mourning" in *Endgame* (Boston: ICA, 1986), p. 47, speculates: "My bet is that the potential for painting will emerge in the conjunctive deconstruction of the three instances which modernist painting has dissociated (the imaginary, the real and the symbolic) but predictions are made to be wrong." Dan Cameron, *The Inconsolable* (New York: Louver Gallery, 1989), p. 5, contends that "it is for the very reason that painting cannot be easily defended in critical terms today that it presents the most likely spawning ground for innovative critical positions." Rainer Crone and David Moos, *Painting Alone* (New York: Pace Gallery, 1990), p. 21, argue: "Painting, if it has the chance to create rather than merely contribute to the cultural discourse, can make pictures about an unfamiliar reality."

34. Benjamin H. D. Buchloh, "Interview with Gerhard Richter" in *Gerhard Richter* (London: Thames and Hudson, 1988), p. 21. Richter continues, "I know for a fact painting is not ineffectual, I would only like it to accomplish more."

35. John McCracken quoted in Anne Ayres, "Connecting Heaven and Earth: The Angelic Madness of John McCracken" in *Heroic Stance: The Sculpture of John McCracken 1965–1986* (Long Island City: PS1, 1986), p. 36.

36. In the 1970s Richard Hamilton proposed a conceptual exhibition in which the catalogue would ultimately preclude the necessity of further realization of the show, a proposal that would doubtless interest Prina.

37. Timothy Martin, "In the Years Preceding 'Olympia': Notes on the Systems Activity of Steve (sic) Prina," *Visions* (Winter 1988), p. 7.

38. George Kubler, *The Shape of Time* (New Haven: Yale University Press, 1962), p. 96.

39. The parallels between Avedon's presentation of this work and nineteenth-century panoramas are striking. Typically, spectators watched an artful recreation of a historical event in an environment where the combination of carefully graduated lighting changes and the slow rotation of the depicted scene heightened the affectivity as well as the illusionism of the portrayal.

40. At the time of writing Derek Jarman's film, *Edward II*, is yet to arrive, bogged down in negotiations between distributors and producers. If film is the most ubiquitous and popular of all the media found here, ironically, on this occasion it has proved most recalcitrant. *Edward II* is scheduled to be shown in Pittsburgh on February 16, 1992.

Michael Asher	Mike Kelley
Richard Avedon	Louise Lawler
Judith Barry	Ken Lum
Lothar Baumgarten	Allan McCollum
Christian Boltanski	John McCracken
Louise Bourgeois	Boris Michailov
John Cage	Lisa Milroy
Sophie Calle	Tatsuo Miyajima
James Coleman	Reinhard Mucha
Tony Cragg	Juan Muñoz
Richard Deacon	Bruce Nauman
Lili Dujourie	Maria Nordman
Katharina Fritsch	Giulio Paolini
Bernard Frize	Stephen Prina
Dan Graham	Tim Rollins + K.O.S.
Ann Hamilton	Richard Serra
Richard Hamilton	Thomas Struth
David Hammons	Hiroshi Sugimoto
Huang Yong Ping	Philip Taaffe
Derek Jarman	Christopher Williams
Ilya Kabakov	Christopher Wool
On Kawara	

Michael Asher

b. 1943, Los Angeles, California, USA

(MSDS) Material Safety Data Sheet
Each chemical product must have a Material Safety Data Sheet, which
can be obtained from the manufacturer, importer, or distributor.
The MSDS is a guide to the safe use and storage of a chemical product.
It includes information regarding hazards relating to ingredients,
physical data, fire, explosion, and health, as well as reactivity, spill and
leak procedures, special protection needed during use, and special
precautions.

(CSA) Center for Safety in the Arts
The Center for Safety in the Arts is a national clearing-house for
research and education on hazards in the visual arts, performing arts,
school art programs, and museums.

Its programs include an Arts Hazards Information Center that responds to inquiries on a daily basis, an educational program that
presents lectures, workshops, and courses on the safe usage of materials, on-site and planning consultations that allow for the inspection
and evaluation of existing and proposed art facilities, and the *Art
Hazards News*, which includes topics such as hazards, precautions,
government regulations, lawsuits, and a calendar of events.

For further information, write the Center for Safety in the Arts, 5
Beekman Street, Suite 1030, New York, NY 10038, or telephone
1-212-227-6220.

(ASTM) American Society for Testing and Materials
The American Society for Testing and Materials is an organization with
members throughout the world who contribute their technical knowledge in order to establish standards for products, systems, materials, and
services that range from paints, metals, textiles, construction, energy,
and consumer products to electronics and computerized systems.

The organization comprises 134 standards-writing committees that
publish standard test methods, specifications, guides, classifications,
and terminology.

The ASTM also publishes the *Annual Book of ASTM Standards.*

(NIOSH) The National Institute for Occupational Safety and Health
The National Institute for Occupational Safety and Health (NIOSH)
conducts research and makes recommendations for the prevention of
work-related illnesses and injuries. NIOSH responds to requests from
employers and employee representatives to evaluate and make recommendations for improving health and safety conditions at workplaces
where hazards are suspected. NIOSH also conducts surveillance of
work-related illnesses and injuries as well as laboratory, industrial
hygiene, intervention, and epidemiologic research. NIOSH publishes
its findings and other current information in bulletins and professional
journals. In addition, NIOSH develops curricula for training industrial
hygienists and other professionals in business, engineering, and medi-
cine. NIOSH transmits its findings and recommendations to the Occupational Safety and Health Administration, which is responsible for
promulgating and enforcing standards. More information about NIOSH
and occupational safety and health concerns is available by calling
NIOSH's toll-free number: 1-800-35-NIOSH.

Installation view

Richard Avedon

b. 1923, New York, New York, USA

Details of **Brandenburg Gate, East Berlin,
New Year's Eve, 1989–1990** 1991

Judith Barry

b. 1949, New York, New York, USA

Ars Memoriae Carnegiensis 1991

Lothar Baumgarten

b. 1944, Rheinsberg, Germany

Grammar of Creation 1990–91

Christian Boltanski

b. 1944, Paris, France

Les Suisses morts (The dead Swiss) 1991

La Réserve du *Carnegie International* **1896–1991** (The archive of the *Carnegie International* 1896–1991) 1991

Louise Bourgeois

b. 1911, Paris, France

Installation view

John Cage

b. 1912, Los Angeles, California, USA

Installation view: days 2, 12, 13, 15, 20, 21, 23, 24,
34, 37, 40, 44

Sophie Calle

b. 1953, Paris, France

Above: Detail of **Last Seen**... 1991

Right: Installation view of **Love Letter** 1988–89

The love letter. 1988

For years a love letter languished on my desk. I had never received a love letter, so I paid a public scribe to write one. Eight days later, I received seven beautiful pages of pure poetry penned in ink. It had cost me one hundred francs and the man said: " as to myself, without moving from my chair I was everywhere with you."

James Coleman

b. 1941, Ballaghaderreen, Co. Roscommon, Ireland

Background 1991

Tony Cragg

b. 1949, Liverpool, England

Top: **Beasts of Burden** 1991
Bottom: **Subcommittee** 1991

Richard Deacon

b. 1949, Bangor, Wales

Installation view

Lili Dujourie

b. 1941, Roeselare, Belgium

Katharina Fritsch

b. 1956, Essen, Germany

Acht Bilder mit Acht Farben
(Eight paintings with eight colors) 1990–91

Bernard Frize

b. 1953, Paris, France

Left: **Mellegers & van der Elsakor** 1989
Center: **63% Vrai** (63% true) 1991
Right: **52% Vrai, 47% Faux**
(52% true, 47% false) 1991

45

Dan Graham

b. 1942, Urbana, Illinois, USA

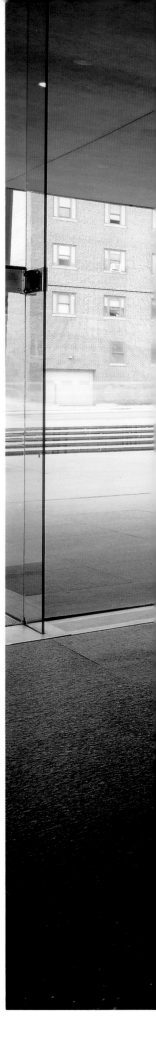

Heart 1991

Ann Hamilton

b. 1956, Lima, Ohio, USA

offerings 1991

Richard Hamilton

b. 1922, London, England

Top: **The Orangeman** 1989–90 and
Lobby 1985–87
Bottom: Installation view

David Hammons

b. 1943, Springfield, Illinois, USA

b. 1943, Springfield, Illinois, USA

Details of **Yo-yo** 1991

Huang Yong Ping

b. 1954, Xiamen, China

Detail of **Unreadable Humidity** 1991

Derek Jarman

b. 1942, Northwood, Middlesex, England

Ilya Kabakov

b. 1933, Dnjepropetrovsk, Ukraine

Detail of **We Are Leaving Here Forever!** 1991

On Kawara

21,483 days (October 19, 1991)

The 1991 Carnegie Prize was awarded to On Kawara
for the installation of *Today, 1966–90.*

The jury who awarded the 1991 Carnegie Prize
was composed of Deborah D. Dodds, Kasper König,
Fumio Nanjo, David Ross, and Konrad M. Weis.

Installation views

Mike Kelley

b. 1954, Detroit, Michigan, USA

Craft Morphology Flow Chart 1991

Louise Lawler

b. 1947, Bronxville, New York, USA

Details of **HAVING ATTAINED VISIBILITY AS
WELL AS MANAGING TO CATCH THE EYE OF
THE SPECTATOR…** 1991

Ken Lum

b. 1956, Vancouver, British Columbia, Canada

Top: Installation view at The Carnegie Museum of Art
Bottom: Installation view at Squirrel Hill Branch
Library

Allan McCollum

b. 1944, Los Angeles, California, USA

Lost Objects 1991

John McCracken

b. 1934, Berkeley, California, USA

Left: **Ra** 1991
Right: **World** 1991

Boris Michailov

b. 1938, Kharkov, Ukraine

Top: **Luriki** 1975–85
Bottom: Installation view

Lisa Milroy

b. 1959, Vancouver, British Columbia, Canada

Left: **Lightbulbs** 1991
Center: **Squares** 1991
Right: **Lightbulbs** 1991

Tatsuo Miyajima

b. 1957, Tokyo, Japan

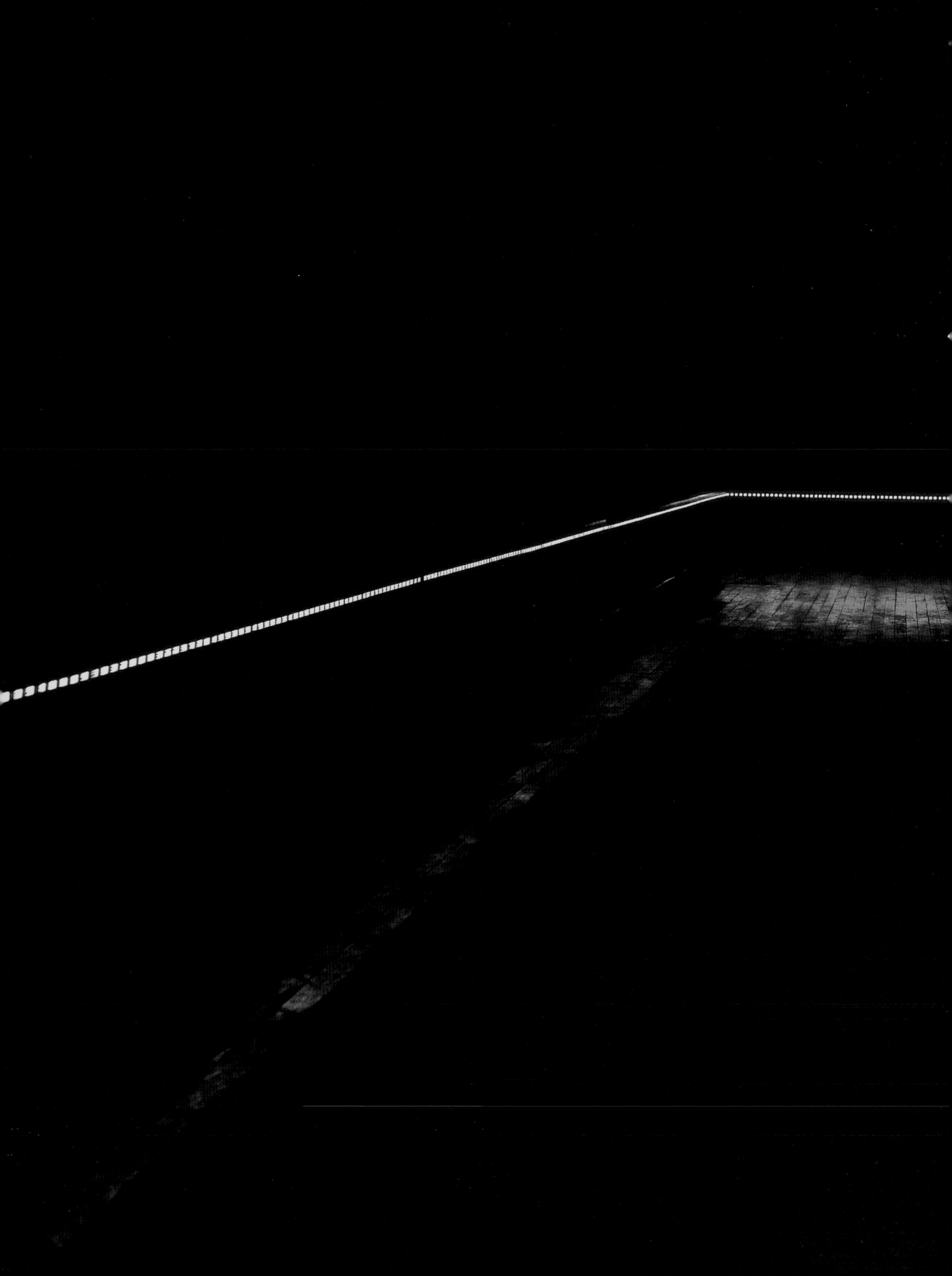

b. 1957, Tokyo, Japan

Over the Border 1991

Reinhard Mucha

b. 1950, Düsseldorf, Germany

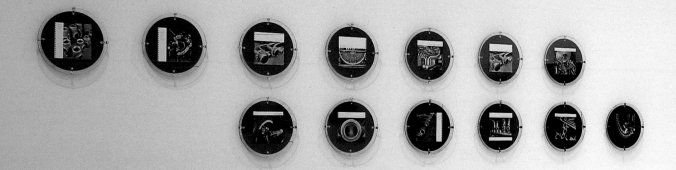

Left: Detail of **The Wirtschaftswunder** 1991
Center: **Oberbilker Markt (OBM)** 1986
Right: **Norden** 1991

Juan Muñoz

b. 1953, Madrid, Spain

Conversation Piece I–V 1991

Bruce Nauman

b. 1941, Fort Wayne, Indiana, USA

Detail of **Untitled** 1991

Maria Nordman

b. 1943, Goerlitz, Germany

Details of **Four Rivers** 1991

73

Giulio Paolini

b. 1940, Genoa, Italy

Detail of **Contemplator Enim** 1991

Stephen Prina

b. 1954, Galesburg, Illinois, USA

Installation view

Tim Rollins + K.O.S.

Checklist

Height precedes width precedes depth, unless otherwise noted.

Michael Asher

Untitled, 1991
Mixed media
Each letter: 7½ in. (19 cm.) high
Courtesy of the artist

Richard Avedon

Brandenburg Gate
East Berlin
New Year's Eve, December 31, 1989–January 1, 1990, 1991
Installation: silver gelatin prints
Installation designed by Richard Avedon, assisted by Mary Shanahan, art director, and Anita Stewart, lighting designer.
192 x 252 x 444 in. (487.7 x 640 x 1127.8 cm.)
Collection of the artist
Courtesy of Eastman Kodak Company, Rochester, and *Egoïste* Magazine, Paris

Judith Barry

Ars Memoriae Carnegiensis, 1991
Mixed media
54 x 14 x 14 in. (137.2 x 35.6 x 35.6 cm.)
Courtesy of the artist and Nicole Klagsbrun Gallery, New York

Lothar Baumgarten

Grammar of Creation, 1990–91
Vinyl on glass
Each letter: 11⅝ in. (29.5 cm.) high
Courtesy of Marian Goodman Gallery, New York

Christian Boltanski

La Réserve du Carnegie International *1896–1991* (The archive of the *Carnegie International* 1896–1991), 1991
Installation: cardboard boxes and lamps
Dimensions variable, here 120 x 780 in. (304.8 x 1981.2 cm.)
Courtesy of Marian Goodman Gallery, New York

Les Suisses morts (The dead Swiss), 1991
Installation: photographs and lamps
216 x 984 in. (548.6 x 2499.4 cm.)
Courtesy of Marian Goodman Gallery, New York

Louise Bourgeois

Cell I, 1991
Mixed media
83 x 96 x 108 in. (210.8 x 243.8 x 274.3 cm.)
Courtesy of Robert Miller Gallery, New York

Cell II, 1991
Mixed media
83 x 60 x 60 in. (210.8 x 152.4 x 152.4 cm.)
The Carnegie Museum of Art, Pittsburgh
Heinz Family Acquisition Fund

Cell III, 1991
Mixed media
111 x 144 x 132 in. (281.9 x 365.8 x 335.3 cm.)
Courtesy of Robert Miller Gallery, New York

Cell IV, 1991
Mixed media
82 x 84 x 84 in. (208.3 x 213.4 x 213.4 cm.)
Courtesy of Robert Miller Gallery, New York

Cell V, 1991
Paint, wood, and metal
92 x 72 x 72 in. (233.7 x 182.9 x 182.9 cm.)
Courtesy of Robert Miller Gallery, New York

Cell VI, 1991
Paint, wood, and metal
63 x 45 x 45 in. (160 x 114.3 x 114.3 cm.)
Courtesy of Robert Miller Gallery, New York

John Cage

Collaboration with Dove Bradshaw, Mary Jean Kenton, and Marsha Skinner

John Cage
Changes and Disappearances No. 20, 1979–81
Color etching
12⅝ x 22⅝ in. (32.1 x 57.5 cm.)
Collection of the artist

Changes and Disappearances No. 21, 1979–81
Color etching
12⅝ x 22⅝ in. (32.1 x 57.5 cm.)
Collection of the artist

Changes and Disappearances No. 29, 1979–81
Color etching
12⅝ x 22⅝ in. (32.1 x 57.5 cm.)
Collection of the artist

(R3) Where R = Ryoanji T.P.f/25, 1983
Drypoint
14¼ x 28¼ in. (36.2 x 72.8 cm.)
Collection of the artist

Eninka No. 20, 1986
Smoked, branded monotype
31¾ x 25¾ in. (80.6 x 65.4 cm.)
Collection of the artist

River Rocks and Smoke No. 11, 1990
Smoke and watercolor on paper
35 x 48⅞ in. (88.9 x 124.1 cm.)
Collection of the artist

Signals 18/25, 1991
Color etching with color plates and 1–5 drawings
13½ x 20⅝ in. (34.3 x 52.4 cm.)
Collection of the artist

Smoke Weather Stone Weather 18/37, 1991
Spitbite aquatint, sugarlift and softground etching on smoked paper
22⅜ x 27⅜ in. (56.8 x 69.5 cm.)
Collection of the artist

Smoke Weather Stone Weather 19/37, 1991
Spitbite aquatint, sugarlift and softground etching on smoked paper
22⅜ x 27⅜ in. (56.8 x 69.5 cm.)
Collection of the artist

Smoke Weather Stone Weather 26/37, 1991
Spitbite aquatint, sugarlift and softground etching
on smoked paper
22⅜ x 27⅜ in. (56.8 x 69.5 cm.)
Collection of the artist

Smoke Weather Stone Weather 36/37, 1991
Spitbite aquatint, sugarlift and softground etching
on smoked paper
22⅜ x 27⅜ in. (56.8 x 69.5 cm.)
Collection of the artist

Smoke Weather Stone Weather 37/37, 1991
Spitbite aquatint, sugarlift and softground etching
on smoked paper
22⅜ x 27⅜ in. (56.8 x 69.5 cm.)
Collection of the artist

Variations II A.P. 8, 1991
Images on smoked paper with irregular branding by
chance operations
32¼ x 26⅜ in. (81.9 x 67 cm.)
Collection of the artist

Variations II A.P. 10, 1991
Images on smoked paper with irregular branding by
chance operations
32¼ x 26⅜ in. (81.9 x 67 cm.)
Collection of the artist

Variations II A.P. 13, 1991
Images on smoked paper with irregular branding by
chance operations
32¼ x 26⅜ in. (81.9 x 67 cm.)
Collection of the artist

Where R = Ryoanji R/5, 1991
Pencil on Japanese paper
16⅝ x 26 in. (42.2 x 66 cm.)
Collection of the artist

Dove Bradshaw

Untitled (Contingency series), 1989–91
Silver leaf and liver of sulfur on paper
32 x 22 in. (81.3 x 55.9 cm.)
Collection of Sarah-Ann and Werner H. Kramarsky

Untitled (Contingency series), 1989–91
Silver leaf and liver of sulfur on paper
32 x 22 in. (81.3 x 55.9 cm.)
Collection of Gordon Douglas

Untitled (Contingency series), 1989–91
Silver leaf and liver of sulfur on paper
32 x 22 in. (81.3 x 55.9 cm.)
Collection of Philip Chiaponne and Mary Brennan

Untitled (Contingency series), 1989–91
Silver leaf and liver of sulfur on paper
32 x 22 in. (81.3 x 55.9 cm.)
Collection of Philip Chiappone and Mary Brennan

Untitled (Contingency series), 1989–91
Silver leaf and liver of sulfur on paper
32 x 22 in. (81.3 x 55.9 cm.)
Collection of John Cage

Untitled (Contingency series), 1989–91
Silver leaf and liver of sulfur on paper
32 x 22 in. (81.3 x 55.9 cm.)
Collection of the artist

Untitled (Contingency series), 1989–91
Silver leaf and liver of sulfur on paper
32 x 22 in. (81.3 x 55.9 cm.)
Collection of the artist

Untitled (Contingency series), 1989–91
Silver leaf and liver of sulfur on paper
32 x 22 in. (81.3 x 55.9 cm.)
Collection of the artist

Untitled (Contingency series), 1989–91
Silver leaf and liver of sulfur on paper
32 x 22 in. (81.3 x 55.9 cm.)
Collection of the artist

Untitled (Contingency series), 1989–91
Silver leaf and liver of sulfur on paper
32 x 22 in. (81.3 x 55.9 cm.)
Collection of the artist

Untitled (Contingency series), 1989–91
Silver leaf and liver of sulfur on paper
32 x 22 in. (81.3 x 55.9 cm.)
Collection of the artist

Untitled (Contingency series), 1989–91
Silver leaf and liver of sulfur on paper
32 x 22 in. (81.3 x 55.9 cm.)
Collection of the artist

Mary Jean Kenton

Nomadic Of Direct Involvement, 1989–90
Watercolor on ragboard
30 x 80 in. (76.2 x 203.2 cm.)
Collection of the artist

Poetry Which Obviously Makes No Sound, 1990
Watercolor on ragboard
30 x 80 in. (76.2 x 203.2 cm.)
Collection of the artist

Travel By Waterway By Conversion Of Earth,
1989–90
Watercolor on ragboard
30 x 80 in. (76.2 x 203.2 cm.)
Collection of the artist

A Sidelong Glance The Venom, 1990
Watercolor on ragboard
30 x 80 in. (76.2 x 203.2 cm.)
Collection of the artist

Unknown Species The Screaming Engine, 1990
Watercolor on ragboard
30 x 80 in. (76.2 x 203.2 cm.)
Collection of John Cage

Handling Reptiles I Remembered, 1990
Watercolor on ragboard
30 x 80 in. (76.2 x 203.2 cm.)
Collection of the artist

*Puts On A Clean Starched Uniform Is A Matter Of
Chance Is Flown*, 1990
Watercolor on ragboard
30 x 60 in. (76.2 x 152.4 cm.)
Collection of the artist

Fence Holes Of The Style Museum, 1990
Watercolor on illustration board
30 x 80 in. (76.2 x 203.2 cm.)
Collection of the artist

Resistance Drawn Up Where The Flowers Inform,
1990
Watercolor on ragboard
30 x 80 in. (76.2 x 203.2 cm.)
Collection of the artist

Tons Of Water Could Be Thrown Aside, 1991
Watercolor on ragboard
30 x 60 in. (76.2 x 152.4 cm.)
Collection of the artist

The Woman The High On The Face Of The Cliff,
1991
Watercolor on ragboard
30 x 60 in. (76.2 x 152.4 cm.)
Collection of the artist

Sheet Of Paper, 1990
Watercolor on illustration board
30 x 80 in. (76.2 x 203.2 cm.)
Collection of the artist

Marsha Skinner

Changes #1, 1991
Oil on canvas
40 x 40 in. (101.6 x 101.6 cm.)
Courtesy of the artist

Changes #2, 1991
Oil on canvas
12 x 12 in. (30.5 x 30.5 cm.)
Courtesy of the artist

Changes #3, 1991
Oil on canvas
12 x 12 in. (30.5 x 30.5 cm.)
Courtesy of the artist

Changes #4, 1991
Oil on canvas
22 x 22 in. (55.9 x 55.9 cm.)
Courtesy of the artist

Changes #5, 1991
Oil on canvas
22 x 22 in. (55.9 x 55.9 cm.)
Courtesy of the artist

Changes #6, 1991
Oil on canvas
48 x 48 in. (121.9 x 121.9 cm.)
Courtesy of the artist

Changes #7, 1991
Oil on canvas
48 x 48 in. (121.9 x 121.9 cm.)
Courtesy of the artist

Changes #8, 1991
Oil on canvas
12 x 12 in. (30.5 x 30.5 cm.)
Courtesy of the artist

Changes #9, 1991
Oil on canvas
40 x 40 in. (101.6 x 101.6 cm.)
Courtesy of the artist

Changes #10, 1991
Oil on canvas
48 x 48 in. (121.9 x 121.9 cm.)
Courtesy of the artist

Changes #11, 1991
Oil on canvas
22 x 22 in. (55.9 x 55.9 cm.)
Courtesy of the artist

Canvas #12, 1991
Oil on canvas
40 x 40 in. (101.6 x 101.6 cm.)
Courtesy of the artist

Sophie Calle

My First Two Photographs, 1978
Two silver gelatin prints
3½ x 2 in. (8.9 x 5.1 cm.)
Collection of the artist

Dutch Portrait, 1988–89
Silver gelatin print
64⅞ x 38⅞ in. (164.8 x 98.7 cm.)
Courtesy of Fred Hoffman Gallery, Santa Monica

Love Letter, 1988–89
Silver gelatin print
11⅞ x 15¾ in. (30 x 40 cm.)
Courtesy of Fred Hoffman Gallery, Santa Monica

Wedding Dress, 1988–89
Silver gelatin print
64⅞ x 38⅞ in. (164.8 x 98.7 cm.)
Courtesy of Fred Hoffman Gallery, Santa Monica

La Fille du docteur (The doctor's daughter), 1991
Silver gelatin print
37½ x 50¼ in. (95.3 x 127 cm.)
Collection of Thea Westreich

Last Seen…, 1991
Nine color photographs plus text
Dimensions variable, here 437½ x 338 in.
(1111.25 x 858.5 cm.)
Collection of the artist

James Coleman

Background, 1991
Multimedia installation
Dimensions variable, here 301 x 264 in.
(764.5 x 670.6 cm.)
The Carnegie Museum of Art, Pittsburgh
Museum purchase: Gift of The Juliet Lea Hillman
Simonds Foundation, Inc. and The Henry L. Hillman
Foundation

Tony Cragg

Beasts of Burden, 1991
Stone
Three parts: 46 x 36 x 68 in.
(116.8 x 91.4 x 172.7 cm.); 30 x 30 x 48 in.
(76.2 x 76.2 x 121.9 cm.); 43 x 25 x 44 in.
(109.2 x 63.5 x 111.8 cm.)
Courtesy of the artist

early forms, 1991
Bronze
Two parts: 65 x 101 x 55 in.
(165.1 x 256.5 x 139.7 cm.); 80 x 102 x 44 in.
(203.2 x 259.1 x 111.8 cm.)
Courtesy of Marian Goodman Gallery, New York

Subcommittee, 1991
Steel
94½ x 78¾ x 33½ in. (240 x 200 x 85 cm.)
Courtesy of Marian Goodman Gallery, New York

Richard Deacon

Facts Not Opinions, 1991
Wood and steel
42½ x 138⅝ x 126¾ in. (108 x 352 x 322 cm.)
(base only)
Courtesy of the artist

Supporting:

Leo Marcotte and Ringuet Le Prince (attributed to)
Center Table, c. 1855–60
Ebonized American black walnut and cherry, ormolu
mounts, and marble
29 x 46 x 34 in. (73.7 x 116.8 x 86.4 cm.)
The Carnegie Museum of Art, Pittsburgh
Museum purchase: Dupuy Fund, 82.30.1

Jean Baptiste Carpeaux
French, 1827–1875
Génie de la danse, c. 1869
Bronze
41¾ x 15 x 13 in. (106 x 38.1 x 33 cm.)
The Carnegie Museum of Art, Pittsburgh
Museum Purchase: Anna R. D. and Mabel Lindsay
Gillespie Fund, 69.52

Gorham Company
Berry Spoon, c. 1883
Silver and gilded silver
10¾ x 2½ in. (27.3 x 6.4 cm.)
The Carnegie Museum of Art, Pittsburgh
Museum Purchase: Gift of Mr. and Mrs. Alexander
C. Speyer, III and the Decorative Arts Purchase
Fund, 88.16

Facts Not Opinions, 1991
Aluminum
11¾ x 118⅛ x 118⅛ in. (30 x 300 x 300 cm.)
(base only)
Courtesy of the artist

Supporting:

Isamu Noguchi
American, 1904–1988
Structure, c. 1945
Wood
53 x 14 x 22 in. (134.6 x 35.6 x 55.9 cm.)
The Carnegie Museum of Art, Pittsburgh
Gift of G. David Thompson, 57.42.7

Gerrit Rietveld
Dutch, 1888–1964
Child's Chair, c. 1920
Wood, deal, and leather
35⅜ x 17 x 17¼ in. (89.9 x 43.2 x 43.8 cm.)
The Carnegie Museum of Art, Pittsburgh
Fellows Fund, 90.20

Owo-eye of Ilesha
Housepost, c. 1930–50
Painted wood
82 x 8¾ x 11 in. (208.3 x 22.2 x 27.9 cm.)
The Carnegie Museum of Art, Pittsburgh
Museum purchase: Gift of the Women's Committee
of the Museum of Art, 77.54

Facts Not Opinions, 1991
Vinyl flooring
102 x 50¾ in. (259 x 129 cm.)
Courtesy of the artist

Supporting:

David Smith
American, 1906–1965
Cubi XXIV, 1964
Stainless steel
114¼ x 83¼ x 32 in. (290.2 x 211.5 x 81.3 cm.)
The Carnegie Museum of Art
Museum Purchase: Gift of Howard Heinz Endow-
ment, 67.6

Lili Dujourie

Caresse, l'horizon de la nuit, 1983
Mixed media
53⅛ x 90½ x 13¾ in. (135 x 230 x 35 cm.)
Collection of Mr. and Mrs. Mark Le Jeune,
Kapellenbos, Belgium

Dimanche après-midi à Berlin, 1990
Marble
Two parts, each 70⅞ x 47¼ in. (180 x 120 cm.)
Courtesy of Galerie Nelson, Lyon

Nature morte no. 3, 1990
Iron and plaster
49⅜ x 34⅝ x 14⅛ in. (125.5 x 88 x 36 cm.)
Collection of Marvin and Elayne Mordes, Baltimore

Katharina Fritsch

*Acht Bilder mit Acht Farben: Rotes Bild, Blaues Bild,
Grünes Bild, Schwarzes Bild, Weisses Bild, Gelbes
Bild, Hellgrünes Bild, Oranges Bild* (Eight paintings
with eight colors: Red painting, blue painting, green
painting, black painting, white painting, yellow paint-
ing, light-green painting, orange painting), 1990–91
Tempera on canvas, wood, metal foil, and gold
lacquer
Each 55⅛ x 39¼ x 3⅜ in. (140 x 100 x 8.5 cm.)
Courtesy Jablonka Galerie, Cologne

Bernard Frize

Mellegers & van der Elsakor, 1989
Dispersion and resin on canvas
94½ x 72¾ in. (240 x 185 cm.)
Courtesy of the artist and Galerie Crousel-Robelin
BAMA, Paris

Extension, 1990
Dispersion and resin on canvas
94½ x 86½ in. (240 x 220 cm.)
Courtesy of the artist and Galerie Crousel-Robelin
BAMA, Paris

63% Vrai (63% true), 1990
Dispersion and resin on canvas
94½ x 86½ in. (240 x 220 cm.)
Courtesy of the artist and Galerie Crousel-Robelin
BAMA, Paris

Oreiller (Pillow), 1991
Dispersion and resin on canvas
94½ x 94½ in. (240 x 240 cm.)
Courtesy of the artist and Galerie Crousel-Robelin
BAMA, Paris

52% Vrai, 47% Faux (52% true, 47% false), 1991
Dispersion and resin on canvas
94½ x 72¾ in. (240 x 185 cm.)
Courtesy of the artist and Galerie Crousel Robelin
BAMA, Paris

Dan Graham

Heart Pavilion, 1991
Two-way mirror glass and steel
94 x 168 x 144 in. (238.7 x 426.7 x 365.8 cm.)
Courtesy of Marian Goodman Gallery, New York

Ann Hamilton

offerings, 1991
Mixed-media installation
Three floors, each 96 x 240 x 360 in.
(243.8 x 609.6 x 914.4 cm.)
Courtesy of the artist and Louver Gallery, New York

Richard Hamilton

The citizen, 1982–83
Oil on canvas
Two canvases, each 78¾ x 39²/₅ in. (200 x 100 cm.)
The Trustees of the Tate Gallery, London
Purchased 1985

OHIO — elevations, 1983
Pen and letrafilm on paper
16½ x 23⅜ in. (42 x 59.4 cm.)
Courtesy of Anthony d'Offay Gallery, London

Diab DS-101, 1983–89
Computer
27½ x 19¹¹/₁₆ x 19¹¹/₁₆ in. (70 x 50 x 50 cm.)
Diab Data AB, Stockholm

Mother and Child, 1984–85
Oil on canvas
59 x 59 in. (150 x 150 cm.)
Collection of Mr. and Mrs. Keith L. Sachs
Courtesy of Anthony d'Offay Gallery, London

Lobby, 1985–87
Oil on canvas
69 x 98⅜ in. (175 x 250 cm.)
Courtesy of Anthony d'Offay Gallery, London

OHIO — axiometric, 1986
Pen and letrafilm on paper
23⅜ x 16½ in. (59.4 x 42 cm.)
Courtesy of Anthony d'Offay Gallery, London

The Orangeman, 1988–90
Oil on canvas
Two canvases, each 78¾ x 39⅜ in. (200 x 100 cm.)
Courtesy of Anthony d'Offay Gallery, London

David Hammons

Yo-yo, 1991
Mixed-media installation
612 x 240 x 216 in. (1554.5 x 609.6 x 548.6 cm.)
Courtesy of the artist

Huang Yong Ping

Unreadable Humidity, 1991
Pulped paper
90 x 295¾ x 28 in. (228.6 x 751.2 x 71.3 cm.)
Courtesy of the artist

Derek Jarman

Edward II, 1991
35mm feature film

Ilya Kabakov

We Are Leaving Here Forever!, 1991
Mixed-media installation
216 x 540 x 540 in. (548.6 x 1371.6 x 1371.6 cm.)
Courtesy of Ronald Feldman Fine Arts, Inc.,
New York

On Kawara

Today, 1966–90, 1991

JANUARY 25, 1966, 1966
Liquitex on canvas
8 x 16½ in. (20.3 x 41.9 cm.)
Courtesy of the artist and Sperone Westwater,
New York

MAY 8, 1967, 1967
Liquitex on canvas
10 x 13 in. (25.4 x 33 cm.)
Courtesy of the artist and Sperone Westwater,
New York

19 JUL. 68, 1968
Liquitex on canvas
10 x 13 in. (25.4 x 33 cm.)
Courtesy of the artist and Sperone Westwater,
New York

24 FEV. 1969, 1969
Liquitex on canvas
10 x 13 in. (25.4 x 33 cm.)
Courtesy of the artist and Sperone Westwater,
New York

24 FEV. 1969, 1969
Liquitex on canvas
10 x 13 in. (25.4 x 33 cm.)
Courtesy of the artist and Sperone Westwater,
New York

MAY 31, 1970, 1970
Liquitex on canvas
13 x 17 in. (33 x 43.1 cm.)
Courtesy of the artist and Sperone Westwater,
New York

OCT. 6, 1971, 1971
Liquitex on canvas
10 x 13 in. (25.4 x 33 cm.)
Courtesy of the artist and Sperone Westwater,
New York

AUG. 17, 1972, 1972
Liquitex on canvas
18 x 24 in. (45.7 x 61 cm.)
Courtesy of the artist and Sperone Westwater,
New York

22 JAN. 1973, 1973
Liquitex on canvas
10 x 13 in. (25.4 x 33 cm.)
Courtesy of the artist and Sperone Westwater,
New York

SEPT. 2, 1974, 1974
Liquitex on canvas
10 x 13 in. (25.4 x 33 cm.)
Courtesy of the artist and Sperone Westwater,
New York

NOV. 5, 1975, 1975
Liquitex on canvas
8 x 10 in. (20.3 x 25.4 cm.)
Courtesy of the artist and Sperone Westwater,
New York

24. MARZ 1976, 1976
Liquitex on canvas
10 x 13 in. (25.4 x 33 cm.)
Courtesy of the artist and Sperone Westwater,
New York

DEC. 13, 1977, 1977
Liquitex on canvas
10 x 13 in. (25.4 x 33 cm.)
Courtesy of the artist and Sperone Westwater,
New York

APR. 27, 1978, 1978
Liquitex on canvas
13 x 17 in. (33 x 43.1 cm.)
Courtesy of the artist and Sperone Westwater,
New York

JUNE 12, 1979, 1979
Liquitex on canvas
10 x 13 in. (25.4 x 33 cm.)
Courtesy of the artist and Sperone Westwater,
New York

FEB. 19, 1980, 1980
Liquitex on canvas
13 x 17 in. (33 x 43.1 cm.)
Courtesy of the artist and Sperone Westwater,
New York

OCT. 30, 1981, 1981
Liquitex on canvas
18 x 24 in. (45.7 x 61 cm.)
Courtesy of the artist and Sperone Westwater,
New York

SEPT. 29, 1982, 1982
Liquitex on canvas
8 x 10 in. (20.3 x 25.4 cm.)
Courtesy of the artist and Sperone Westwater,
New York

DEC. 12, 1983, 1983
Liquitex on canvas
10 x 13 in. (25.4 x 33 cm.)
Courtesy of the artist and Sperone Westwater,
New York

4 AUG. 1984, 1984
Liquitex on canvas
10 x 13 in. (25.4 x 33 cm.)
Courtesy of the artist and Sperone Westwater,
New York

JUNE 1, 1985, 1985
Liquitex on canvas
10 x 13 in. (25.4 x 33 cm.)
Courtesy of the artist and Sperone Westwater,
New York

APR. 14, 1986, 1986
Liquitex on canvas
10 x 13 in. (25.4 x 33 cm.)
Courtesy of the artist and Sperone Westwater,
New York

NOV. 20, 1987, 1987
Liquitex on canvas
18 x 24 in. (45.7 x 61 cm.)
Courtesy of the artist and Sperone Westwater,
New York

FEB. 29, 1988, 1988
Liquitex on canvas
13 x 17 in. (33 x 43.1 cm.)
Courtesy of the artist and Sperone Westwater,
New York

16. JAN. 1989, 1989
Liquitex on canvas
10 x 13 in. (25.4 x 33 cm.)
Walker Art Center, Minneapolis
T. B. Walker Acquisition Fund, 1991

17. JAN. 1989, 1989
Liquitex on canvas
10 x 13 in. (25.4 x 33 cm.)
Walker Art Center, Minneapolis
T. B. Walker Acquisition Fund, 1991

18. JAN. 1989, 1989
Liquitex on canvas
10 x 13 in. (25.4 x 33 cm.)
Walker Art Center, Minneapolis
T. B. Walker Acquisition Fund, 1991

19. JAN. 1989, 1989
Liquitex on canvas
10 x 13 in. (25.4 x 33 cm.)
Walker Art Center, Minneapolis
T. B. Walker Acquisition Fund, 1991

20. JAN. 1989, 1989
Liquitex on canvas
10 x 13 in. (25.4 x 33 cm.)
Walker Art Center, Minneapolis
T. B. Walker Acquisition Fund, 1991

13 GEN. 1990, 1990
Liquitex on canvas
10 x 13 in. (25.4 x 33 cm.)
Courtesy of the artist and Sperone Westwater,
New York

APR. 4, 1990, 1990
Liquitex on canvas
10 x 13 in. (25.4 x 33 cm.)
Courtesy of the artist and Sperone Westwater,
New York

6 JUL. 1990, 1990
Liquitex on canvas
10 x 13 in. (25.4 x 33 cm.)
Courtesy of the artist and Sperone Westwater,
New York

AUG. 26, 1990, 1990
Liquitex on canvas
10 x 13 in. (25.4 x 33 cm.)
Courtesy of the artist and Sperone Westwater,
New York

27 OTT. 1990, 1990
Liquitex on canvas
10 x 13 in. (25.4 x 33 cm.)
Courtesy of the artist and Sperone Westwater,
New York

5 NOV. 1990, 1990
Liquitex on canvas
10 x 13 in. (25.4 x 33 cm.)
Courtesy of the artist and Sperone Westwater,
New York

Mike Kelley

Craft Morphology Flow Chart, 1991
Mixed-media installation
Dimensions variable, here 568¾ x 528 in.
(1444.6 x 1341.1 cm.)
Courtesy of the artist, Anthony d'Offay Gallery,
London, and Rosamund Felsen Gallery, Santa Monica

Louise Lawler

HAVING ATTAINED VISIBILITY AS WELL AS
MANAGING TO CATCH THE EYE OF THE
SPECTATOR..., 1991
Three color photographs, paint and paperweight,
letterform design by Tony Di Spigna
Varying dimensions, each photograph 24 x 20 in.
(61 x 50.8 cm.)
The Carnegie Museum of Art, Pittsburgh
A. W. Mellon Acquisition Endowment Fund

Ken Lum

Selected Inuit Poem
Allegheny Branch, Carnegie Library, Pittsburgh,
U.S.A.
Call no.: E 99 .E7 W72 1983
Ken Lum Personal Library, Vancouver, 1991
Oil and acrylic on canvas, wooden dowels
150 x 90 in. (381 x 228.6 cm.)
Courtesy of the artist and Andrea Rosen Gallery,
New York

Selected Japanese Poem
Knoxville Branch, Carnegie Library, Pittsburgh,
U.S.A.
Call no.: PL 729 .F83 1989
Osaka Furitsu Naknoshimo Toshokan Library,
Osaka, Japan
Call no.: Cultural Science Department, Poetry 224,
226/1175, 1991
Oil and acrylic on canvas and wooden dowels
150 x 90 in. (381 x 228.6 cm.)
Courtesy of the artist and Andrea Rosen Gallery,
New York

Selected Maltese Poem
East Liberty Branch, Carnegie Library, Pittsburgh,
U.S.A.
Call no.: PJ 8454 .I44 1989x
National Library, Valletta, Malta
Call no.: 313953, 1991
Oil and acrylic on canvas and wooden dowels
150 x 90 in. (381 x 228.6 cm.)
Courtesy of the artist and Andrea Rosen Gallery,
New York

Selected Nepalese Poem
Mount Washington Branch, Carnegie Library,
Pittsburgh, U.S.A.
Call no.: PK 2598 .L44 T3 1988x
Central Library, Katmandu, Kingdom of Nepal
Call no.: 73002, 1991
Oil and acrylic on canvas and wooden dowels
150 x 90 in. (381 x 228.6 cm.)
Courtesy of the artist and Andrea Rosen Gallery,
New York

Selected Vietnamese Poem
Allegheny Regional Branch, Carnegie Library,
Pittsburgh, U.S.A.
Call no.: Pl 4382 .E3 C3
Sedgewick Library, University of British Columbia,
Vancouver
Call no.: Pl 4382E3 H471991, 1991
Oil and acrylic on canvas and wooden dowels
150 x 90 in. (381 x 228.6 cm.)
Courtesy of the artist and Andrea Rosen Gallery,
New York

Allan McCollum

Lost Objects, 1991
Enamel on cast concrete
22 x 285 x 864 in. (55.9 x 723.9 x 2194.6 cm.)
Courtesy of the artist and John Weber Gallery,
New York

John McCracken

Arrow, 1991
Pigmented polyester resin, fiberglass, and plywood
20½ x 230 x 14 in. (52 x 584.2 x 35.6 cm.)
Courtesy of Fred Hoffman Gallery, Santa Monica

Ra, 1991
Pigmented polyester resin, fiberglass, and plywood
21¼ x 230 x 14 in. (54 x 584.2 x 35.6 cm.)
Courtesy of Fred Hoffman Gallery, Santa Monica

World, 1991
Pigmented polyester resin, fiberglass, and plywood
11¼ x 665 x 19 in. (28.6 x 1689.1 x 48.3 cm.)
Courtesy of Fred Hoffman Gallery, Santa Monica

Boris Michailov

From the series *Luriki*, 1975–85
Thirty-two hand-colored found photographs
Each 20¼ x 15¼ in. (51.4 x 38.7 cm.)
Collection of the artist

From the series *Sots Art*, 1975–85
Five hand-painted found photographs
Varying dimensions
Collection of the artist

From the series *Berdyansk, The Beach*, 1980
Fourteen black and white photographs
Each 23 x 17 in. (58.4 x 43.2 cm.)
Collection of the artist

From the series *Kharkov*, 1990–
Seventy-two sepia-toned photographs
Each 5¼ x 11¼ in. (13.3 x 28.5 cm.)
Collection of the artist

Lisa Milroy

Books, 1991
Oil on canvas
76 x 112 in. (193 x 284.4 cm.)
Collection of the artist

Lightbulbs, 1991
Oil on canvas
86 x 117 in. (218.4 x 297.2 cm.)
Collection of the artist

Lightbulbs, 1991
Oil on canvas
80 x 102 in. (203.2 x 259 cm.)
Collection of the artist

Squares, 1991
Oil on canvas
80 x 144 in. (203.2 x 365.7 cm.)
Collection of the artist

Squares, 1991
Oil on canvas
76 x 102 in. (193 x 259 cm.)
Collection of the artist

Tatsuo Miyajima

Over the Border, 1991
Mixed-media installation: light-emitting diodes,
integrated circuit, electric wire, and wood panel
Dimensions of room: 144 x 424¾ x 796⅞ in.
(365.8 x 1079 x 2024 cm.)
Courtesy of Gallery Takagi, Nagoya, and Luhring
Augustine Gallery, New York

Reinhard Mucha

Untitled (Wand), 1985
Wood, linoleum, felt, aluminum, glass, paint,
photographs, and drawing
51¼ x 110¼ x 7⅞ in. (130 x 280 x 20 cm.)
Collection of Micheline and Charly Szwajcer,
Antwerp

Eslohe, 1986
Door, wood, felt, glass, and aluminum
37⅜ x 78¾ x 15¾ in. (95 x 200 x 40 cm.)
Courtesy of Galleria Lia Rumma, Naples

Flinger Broich (Billiard table), 1986
Pool table, wood, felt, and paint on glass
48 x 83 x 14 in. (121.9 x 210.8 x 35.5 cm.)
Collection of Emily and Jerry Spiegel, New York

Oberbilker Markt (OBM), 1986
Wood, canvas, and artificial resin
47¼ x 86½ x 19¼ in. (120 x 219.7 x 49 cm.)
Collection of O. M. Ungers

Norden, 1991
Wood, aluminum, glass, and felt
43¾ x 87¾ x 10⅝ in. (111 x 223 x 27 cm.)
Collection of Vijak Mahdavi and Bernardo Nadal
Ginard, Boston

The Wirtschaftswunder, 1991
To the People of Pittsburgh
Aluminum, glass, felt, synthetic resin lacquer, and
pages from book
Sixteen elements, each 15¼ in. (38.5 cm.) in
diameter; distance to the wall 1¾ in. (4.2 cm.)
Private collection, Düsseldorf

Juan Muñoz

Conversation Piece I–V, 1991
Bronze
Each 27½ x 28 x 15¾ in. (70 x 71 x 40 cm.)
Courtesy of Marian Goodman Gallery, New York

Bruce Nauman

Untitled, 1991
Bronze, wax, resin, rebar, wire, cardboard, and wood
Dimensions variable, here 276 x 551 in.
(701 x 1399.5 cm.)
Courtesy of Leo Castelli Gallery, New York, and
Sperone Westwater, New York

Maria Nordman

*Four Rivers: Penn and Liberty Avenues at Stanwix
Street 1991–*, 1991
Arbor Vitae, Ginkgo Biloba, Kornus Koussa trees,
steel, and water
260 x 220 ft. (79 x 67 m.)
Courtesy of the artist

Giulio Paolini

Contemplator Enim, 1991
Twenty drawings: collage, pencil on paper, and
photographs
Each 9 x 12³/₅ in. (23 x 32 cm.)
Courtesy of Galleria Christian Stein, Turin and Milan

Contemplator Enim (studies), 1991
Seven drawings: collage, pencil on paper, and
photographs
Each 27³/₅ x 19⁷/₁₀ in. (70 x 50 cm.)
Courtesy of Galleria Christian Stein, Turin and Milan

Stephen Prina

*"The history of modern painting, to label it with a
phrase, has been the struggle against the catalogue..."
— Barnett Newman/(Monochrome Painting,
1988–89)*, 1991
Ink on wash rag, barrier paper, and cardboard
Dimensions variable, here 376½ x 338 in.
(956.3 x 858.5 cm.)
Courtesy of the artist and Luhring Augustine
Gallery, New York

Tim Rollins + K.O.S.

K.O.S. 1990–91:
Angel Abreu
Jorge Abreu
Christopher Hernandez
Victor Llanos
Nelson Montes
Carlos Rivera
Nelson Savinon
Lenin Tejada

Pittsburgh students who collaborated on *The
Temptation of Saint Antony — The Forms*, 1991:
Chad Bartlett
Elise DeLuca
Brian Doyle
Thom Dunn
Lori Goehring
Derek Glover
Kathy Kranack
Emily Krill
Giulia Loli
Simon Lund
Beth McClore
Mika Naatsura
Rick Peelor
Mike Rock
Karen Scanlon
Patricia Stone
Matt Taylor
Bryan Yourick

Twenty-One Books for the People of Homewood,
1990–91
Mixed media in twenty-one books
Varying dimensions
The Carnegie Library of Pittsburgh
Gift of Tim Rollins + K.O.S

The Temptation of Saint Antony — The Forms,
1991
Blood, alcohol, and ink on paper, linen on wood
panels, and matte medium
25 x 228 in. (63.5 x 579.1 cm.)
The Carnegie Museum of Art, Pittsburgh
Gift Fund for Specific Acquisitions

Richard Serra

Judith and Holofernes, 1991
Paintstick on Belgian linen
Two elements, each 132 x 504 in.
(335.3 x 1280.2 cm.)
Courtesy of the artist

Thomas Struth

Hoher Weg, Essen 4/10, 1984
C-Print
26 x 33 in. (66 x 84 cm.)
Courtesy of Marian Goodman Gallery, New York

Kanzlerstrasse, Duisburg 5/10, 1989
Silver gelatin print
26 x 33 in. (66 x 84 cm.)
Courtesy of Marian Goodman Gallery, New York

Leipziger Strasse, Essen 8/10, 1989
Silver gelatin print
26 x 33 in. (66 x 84 cm.)
Courtesy of Marian Goodman Gallery, New York

Pantheon, Rome 4/10, 1990
C-Print
72¼ x 93¾ in. (183.5 x 238 cm.)
Courtesy of Marian Goodman Gallery, New York

Piazza San Ignazio I–III, Rome 2/10, 1990
Three silver gelatin prints
Each 26 x 33 in. (66 x 84 cm.)
Courtesy of Marian Goodman Gallery, New York

South Kimbark Avenue, Chicago 2/10, 1990
Silver gelatin print
26 x 33 in. (66 x 84 cm.)
Courtesy of Marian Goodman Gallery, New York

South Lake Street Apartments I–IV, Chicago
8/10, 1990
Four silver gelatin prints
Each 27½ x 33 in. (70 x 84 cm.)
Courtesy of Marian Goodman Gallery, New York

Ackerstrasse, Düsseldorf 1/10, 1991
Silver gelatin print
26 x 33 in. (66 x 84 cm.)
Courtesy of Marian Goodman Gallery, New York

Shibuya Crossing, Tokyo 3/10, 1991
C-Print
72½ x 95 in. (184 x 241.3 cm.)
Courtesy of Marian Goodman Gallery, New York

Traditional Japanese House, Yamaguchi 3/10, 1991
Silver gelatin print
26 x 33 in. (66 x 84 cm.)
Courtesy of Marian Goodman Gallery, New York

Hiroshi Sugimoto

Time Exposed, 1991

Mediterranean Sea: La Ciotat 1989
Atlantic Ocean: Cliffs of Moher 1989
Atlantic Ocean: Cliffs of Moher 1989
English Channel: Fécamp 1989
Mediterranean Sea: Cassis 1989
Mediterranean Sea: Cassis 1989
South Pacific Ocean: Maraenui 1990
Arctic Ocean: Nord Kapp 1990
Arctic Ocean: Nord Kapp 1990
Irish Sea: Isle of Man 1990
Irish Sea: Isle of Man 1990
Tyrrhenian Sea: Amalfi 1990
Adriatic Sea: Gargano 1990
Ionian Sea: Santa Cesarea 1990
Ionian Sea: Santa Cesarea 1990
Ionian Sea: Santa Cesarea 1990
Mediterranean Sea: Crete 1990
Aegean Sea: Pilion 1990
Aegean Sea: Pilion 1990
Aegean Sea: Pilion 1990
Mirtoan Sea: Sounion 1990
Mirtoan Sea: Sounion 1990
Indian Ocean: Bali 1991
Java Sea: Bali 1991
South Pacific Ocean: Taerai 1991

Silver gelatin prints, wall, and water
Dimensions variable, each photograph 20 x 24 in.
(50.8 x 61 cm.)
Courtesy of the artist

Philip Taaffe

Arcade, 1990
Mixed media on linen
76⅜ x 185¼ in. (194 x 470.5 cm.)
Collection of the artist

Al Qasbah, 1991
Mixed media on linen
90 x 181 in. (228.6 x 459.7 cm.)
Courtesy of Gagosian Gallery, New York

Herculaneum, 1991
Mixed media on linen
112 x 145 in. (284.5 x 368.3 cm.)
Courtesy of Gagosian Gallery, New York

Zone of the Straits, 1991
Mixed media on linen
114 x 114 in. (289.6 x 289.6 cm.)
Courtesy of Gagosian Gallery, New York

Christopher Williams

(Supplement* 1)
Cyprus 1/8, 1990
1785
8809
Burhinus Oedicnemus
Stone Curlew
Burhinidae
9.11.82
Presented by Philip Wayre,
Norfolk Wildlife Park, Great Britain
Edition size: 8 and 5 artist's proofs
Artist book, vitrine of apple maple plywood,
½-inch untempered glass, and Arten temperature
humidity meter
Book, 34 x 32 in. (86.4 x 81.3 cm.); vitrine,
43⅜ x 73⅜ x 38 in. (110.2 x 186.4 x 96.5 cm.)
Collection of Gaby and Wilhelm Schürmann,
Herzogenrath, Germany

(Supplement* 2)
Guinea 2/8, 1990
1358
14069
Otus Leucotis
White-faced Scops Owl
Strigidae
14.7.88
Hatched in the London Zoo,
Regent's Park, London, Great Britain
Edition Size: 8 and 5 artist's proofs
Artist book, vitrine of apple maple plywood,
½-inch untempered glass, and Arten temperature
humidity meter
Book, 34 x 32 in. (86.4 x 81.3 cm.); vitrine,
43⅜ x 73⅜ x 38 in. (110.2 x 186.4 x 96.5 cm.)
Courtesy of Luhring Augustine Hetzler Gallery,
Santa Monica

(Supplement* 3)
Iran 3/8, 1990
2180
763
Francolinus Pondicerianus
Indian Francolin
Phasianidae
23.7.85
Presented by Mr. R. Ahmed
Edition size: 8 and 5 artist's proofs
Artist book, vitrine of apple maple plywood,
½-inch untempered glass, and Arten temperature
humidity meter
Book, 34 x 32 in. (86.4 x 81.3 cm.); vitrine,
43⅜ x 73⅜ x 38 in. (110.2 x 186.4 x 96.5 cm.)
Courtesy of Luhring Augustine Hetzler Gallery,
Santa Monica

(Supplement* 4)
Iraq 4/8, 1990
2128
15141
Pterocles Alchata
Pintailed Sandgrouse
Pteroclididae
18.11.88
Presented by Cardiff University
Cardiff, Wales
Edition size: 8 and 5 artist's proofs
Artist book, vitrine of apple maple plywood,
½-inch untempered glass, and Arten temperature
humidity meter
Book, 34 x 32 in. (86.4 x 81.3 cm.); vitrine,
43⅜ x 73⅜ x 38 in. (110.2 x 186.4 x 96.5 cm.)
Courtesy of Luhring Augustine Hetzler Gallery,
Santa Monica

(Supplement* 5)
Morocco 5/8, 1990
2128
15141
Pterocles Alchata
Pintailed Sandgrouse
Pteroclididae
18.11.88
Presented by Cardiff University
Cardiff, Wales
Edition size: 8 and 5 artist's proofs
Artist book, vitrine of apple maple plywood,
½-inch untempered glass, and Arten temperature
humidity meter
Book, 34 x 32 in. (86.4 x 81.3 cm.); vitrine,
43⅜ x 73⅜ x 38 in. (110.2 x 186.4 x 96.5 cm.)
Courtesy of Luhring Augustine Hetzler Gallery,
Santa Monica

(Supplement* 6)
Nepal 6/8, 1990
96
8679
Gracula Religiosa Intermedia
Nepal Hill Myna
Archie
Sturnidae
10.3.878
Presented by Mrs. Lewis
Edition size: 8 and 5 artist's proofs
Artist book, vitrine of apple maple plywood,
½-inch untempered glass, and Arten temperature
humidity meter
Book, 34 x 32 in. (86.4 x 81.3 cm.); vitrine,
43⅜ x 73⅜ x 38 in. (110.2 x 186.4 x 96.5 cm.)
Courtesy of Luhring Augustine Hetzler Gallery,
Santa Monica

(Supplement* 7)
Seychelles 7/8, 1990
1730
3657
Threskiornis Aethiopica
Sacred Ibis
Threkiornithidae
12.6.79
Hatched in the London Zoo,
Regent's Park, London, Great Britain
Edition size: 8 and 5 artist's proofs
Artist book, vitrine of apple maple plywood,
½-inch untempered glass, and Arten temperature
humidity meter
Book, 34 x 32 in. (86.4 x 81.3 cm.); vitrine,
43⅜ x 73⅜ x 38 in. (110.2 x 186.4 x 96.5 cm.)
Courtesy of Luhring Augustine Hetzler Gallery,
Santa Monica

(Supplement* 8)
Zaire 8/8, 1990
198
4666
Quela Quela
Red-Billed Weaver
Ploceidae
15.10.76
Gift to Society from Mr. T. F. Martin
Edition size: 8 and 5 artist's proofs
Artist book, vitrine of apple maple plywood,
½-inch untempered glass, and Arten temperature
humidity meter
Book, 34 x 32 in. (86.4 x 81.3 cm.); vitrine,
43⅜ x 73⅜ x 38 in. (110.2 x 186.4 x 96.5 cm.)
Courtesy of Luhring Augustine Hetzler Gallery,
Santa Monica

Supplement A.P. 1/5, 1990
Artist's book, 34 x 32 in. (86.4 x 81.3 cm.)

Supplement A.P. 2/5, 1990
Artist's book, 34 x 32 in. (86.4 x 81.3 cm.)

Supplement A.P. 3/5, 1990
Artist's book, 34 x 32 in. (86.4 x 81.3 cm.)

Supplement A.P. 4/5, 1990
Artist's book, 34 x 32 in. (86.4 x 81.3 cm.)

Supplement A.P. 5/5, 1990
Artist's book, 34 x 32 in. (86.4 x 81.3 cm.)

Vitrine, 45¼ x 51 x 37 in. (115 x 129.5 x 94 cm.)
Courtesy of Luhring Augustine Hetzler Gallery,
Santa Monica

Christopher Wool

Untitled, 1991
Enamel on aluminum
277½ x 180 in. (704.8 x 457.2 cm.)
Courtesy of the artist

Untitled, 1991
Two-sided billboard: enamel on plywood
96 x 288 in. (243.8 x 731.5 cm.)
Courtesy of the artist

Plan

*Indicates installation at Mattress Factory
†Indicates off-site installation

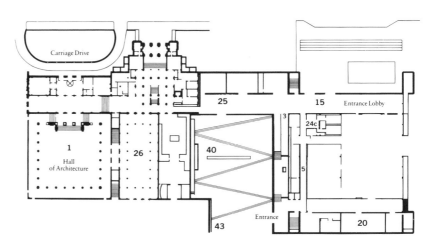

First Floor

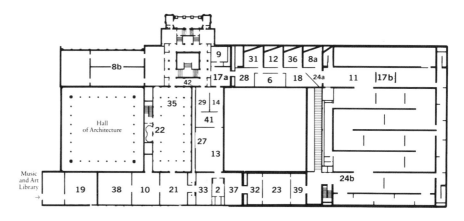

Second Floor

Photograph Credits